Children's Perspectives on Believing and Belonging

Available in alternative formats

This publication can be provided in alternative formats, such as large print, Braille, audiotape and on disk. Please contact: Communications Department, Joseph Rowntree Foundation, The Homestead, 40 Water End, York YO30 6WP. Tel: 01904 615905. Email: info@jrf.org.uk

Children's Perspectives on Believing and Belonging

Greg Smith

Joseph Rowntree Foundation

The Joseph Rowntree Foundation has supported this project as part of its programme of research and innovative development projects, which it hopes will be of value to policy-makers, practitioners and service users.

National Children's Bureau

NCB promotes the voices, interests and well-being of all children and young people across every aspect of their lives. As an umbrella body for the children's sector in England and Northern Ireland, NCB provides essential information on policy, research and best practice for its members and other partners.

NCB aims to:

- challenge disadvantage in childhood
- work with children and young people to ensure they are involved in all matters that affect their lives
- promote multidisciplinary cross-agency partnership and good practice
- influence government through policy development and advocacy
- undertake high quality research and work from an evidence-based perspective
- disseminate information to all those working with children and young people, and to children and young people themselves.

The views expressed in this book are those of the author and not necessarily those of the National Children's Bureau, the Joseph Rowntree Foundation or the Centre for Institutional Studies, University of East London.

Published by the National Children's Bureau for the Joseph Rowntree Foundation

National Children's Bureau, 8 Wakley Street, London EC1V 7QE
Tel: 020 7843 6000
Website: www.ncb.org.uk
Registered Charity Number: 258825

© Centre for Institutional Studies, University of East London 2005

Published 2005

ISBN 1 904787 53 3

British Library Cataloguing in Publication Data
A catalogue record for this book is available from the British Library

Contents

Acknowledgements

We would like to thank the many people without whom this research would not have been possible.

We begin with the most important, about 100 children from three different schools who enthusiastically took part in the project and shared their experiences, opinions and time with us. In fact, the relationships that we built with these children have made this one of the most enjoyable and rewarding research projects that we have worked on.

We are also grateful for the cooperation and involvement of the heads, teachers and other staff of the three schools in which we carried out the fieldwork. In the midst of busy and stressful professional lives and working under the pressures to perform to the high standards measured by the SATs league tables, they without exception showed interest, courtesy and support for our work.

The staff of the Joseph Rowntree Foundation were a source of encouragement and support and did everything to make our task easier. We would also like to thank the members of the Project's Advisory Group (listed below), who offered valuable advice throughout the research project. In addition, a number of people who had special expertise because of their experience within, or study of, Muslim communities read the manuscript and offered comments at the final stage before publication. We are particularly grateful in this respect to Anjum Anwar of the Lancashire Council of Mosques, and Bill Gent, RE Adviser of the London Borough of Redbridge.

Our colleagues at the Centre for Institutional Studies, University of East London (UEL) and staff from the University of Manchester were always supportive. A special thank you goes to Irene Smith who made sure that the administration of the dispersed team always ran smoothly. We must acknowledge the support of our personal social networks, which include families and friends, without which we could not have completed the task.

The Research Team consisted of Greg Smith, who worked throughout the project in design, fieldwork in three schools and data analysis and was responsible for the drafting of the final report, Andri Soteri-Proctor, who worked for 18 months on the project in the design, part of the data analysis and fieldwork in two schools, and Afsia Khanom, who worked mainly on interviewing and transcription in one of the schools. All three were based at the Centre for Institutional Studies, University of East London.

The Project Advisory Group consists of the Chair, Susan Taylor, Joseph Rowntree Foundation, and the members: Paul Butler, Church of England, Sangeeta Chattoo, University of Leeds, Kathryn Copsey, Children in Urban Situations (CURBS) Project, Elaine Kennedy, Department for Education and Skills, Charlotte Hardman, University of Newcastle, Berry Mayall, University of London Institute of Education, Ginny Morrow, Brunel University, Eleanor Nesbitt, Religions and Education Research Unit, University of Warwick, Mike Hornsby-Smith, University of Surrey, Keith J White, Mill Grove/Spurgeons College, and Mustafa Draper, University of Birmingham.

Summary: children's perspectives on believing and belonging

This study, carried out by a team from the University of East London, involved just over 100 children aged 9 to 11, from a wide range of religious backgrounds, in three schools in multi-ethnic inner city areas in the North of England and London. Using in-depth interviews, mostly with pairs of children, supported by a range of other classroom-based data gathering methods, the researchers sought to ascertain children's perspectives on the role (if any) that religion plays in their own and other children's lives, in the context of religiously diverse schools and local communities.

Key findings

Children's patterns of religious observance were not strictly and simply related to religious affiliation or being labelled as an adherent of one of the 'world religions'. Rather, they emerged in the context of a complex pattern of identity and belonging which might involve among other things kinship, ethnicity, age and gender.

Within each of the various religious affiliation groups there were children with different levels and patterns of both the social observance of their religion and the personal commitment to and understanding of faith. Within our sample there was a tendency for the Muslim children to be at the more observant end of the spectrum and white children to be at the least observant end.

Children appreciated that primary schools (regardless of their religious status) played a role in bringing children of different religions together. Many of them valued the opportunity to mix across cultures and learn about these differences. However, despite official commitment to valuing diversity, some school policies and practices reinforced informal segregation and, in some children's views, failed to deal adequately with conflicts between groups marked by religious/ethnic difference. There were some issues where some children felt that they and their religion were not being treated fairly.

School is a setting which allows friendships between children of different backgrounds to develop. However, identity issues, in which religion may play a part within locally specific ethnic group dynamics, mean there are divisions and conflicts which children recognise.

Gender and age group seem to play a greater part than religion or ethnicity in shaping children's friendship patterns at school. Religious identity and personal faith are not in themselves a barrier to friendship. However, cross-cultural networks often did not continue into other contexts such as the home or neighbourhood. Children recognise this is in part the result of very different lifestyles that are shaped by religious and cultural differences, especially between highly observant children (who in our sample were mostly Muslim) and less observant children.

1. Introduction

Policy and research background

There is a large and growing amount of academic, policy and action-led research about children. The Joseph Rowntree Foundation Research Programme on Understanding Children's Lives, of which this project is part, aims to extend this field of knowledge. Briefly, before the 1980s much of the western literature talked about a child as 'becoming a person' and children were often described as passive beings developed and shaped by their environment. During more recent decades such ideas have been challenged with perspectives emerging around the idea that a child is a person in their own right and that children, to a greater or lesser extent, like adults, are reflective social actors able to interact, negotiate and participate in constructing and reconstructing their social environment (for further discussions about this see Hill and Tisdall 1997; James and others 1998; Smart and others 2001; Mayall 2002).

In recent years, much research has been undertaken to examine children's perspectives about how they understand and experience a wide range of issues across their lives, including: family life (Smart and others 2001); health and education (for examples see Hill and Tisdall 1997); gender; class and ethnicity (Connolly 1998); bullying (Eslea and Mukhtaar 2000); and on children's networks and neighbourhoods (Morrow 2001; Christensen and others 2003). Researchers have also studied children and religion for educational purposes. Much of this has examined children in the context of a single specific religion, and includes such work as *Hindu Children in Britain* (Jackson and Nesbitt 1993), Nesbitt's work on Sikh children (2000), and Parker-Jenkins' (1995) on Muslim children. Ericker and others (2001) have looked more comparatively at children's spirituality. However, there is a substantial gap of research about the social experience of young children and their interactions across different religions.

The focus of this research project was to explore and examine children's views and perspectives of their own and/or other children's religion, and the extent to which religion contributes to shaping personal identities and social and friendship networks. This research has relevance not only to those interested in the lives of children, but also at a wider policy level, where current debates about social cohesion, 'faith-based' schools and the potential resources of 'faith communities' are taking place. In this policy discourse religious institutions are seen, on the one hand, as contributing to building networks within and across communities and, on the other hand, as contributing to defining and segregating communities (Cantle 2001; Farnell and others 2003).

Research questions

The research aimed to understand issues about religion by examining children's accounts and perspectives across different sections of their lives. The ambition of the project was to address four main research questions:

- How (if at all) do children talk about issues of belief and their own individual faith and how do they describe the social aspects of religion in their own and other people's lives?
- How do children talk about religious belonging as part of their own and/or other people's identity and social resources, in a complex social context where ethnicity, language, gender, age and social class also play a part?
- How do the various religious elements of life manifest themselves in children's lives (in the spheres of school, friendship networks, neighbourhood and family, and formal religious institutions)?
- Is it possible to detect any childhood-based evidence of segregation of communities defined by religion into parallel but unconnected social universes?

The limitations of this report format mean we can only cover the most significant discoveries made in the course of the research. We hope that further analysis and more detailed publications on particular topics will follow.

Research design and fieldwork setting

Localities

The study involved children between the ages of 9 and 11 in the final two years of primary schooling. Time and resource constraints inevitably influenced the research design, and selection of locations and schools depended on a number of factors. First, it was important that the geographical areas selected had diverse multi-ethnic and multi-faith populations, to enable the researchers to draw on a range of children from different cultural backgrounds. Second, due to time, travel and resource constraints, we decided to build on the research team's existing local networks. As a result, two inner city neighbourhoods, one in London and one in the North of England, were selected. For purposes of maintaining the schools' and children's anonymity we do not disclose the exact locations of these areas, and throughout the rest of this report we refer to the areas as Eastborough and Northcity respectively. Two schools from Northcity and one in Eastborough were approached for this study, and all agreed to participate.

The two schools in Northcity are located in wards where poverty and deprivation are prevalent. These wards are ranked in the bottom 5 and 20 per cent of the government index of local deprivation for 2000. According to the 2001 census, approximately 15 per cent of Northcity's population is from ethnic minority backgrounds, this rises to 37 and 26 per cent in the wards where the research took place. Most defined themselves as Indian (9 per cent) or Pakistani (2 per cent).

In the wards where we worked the (voluntary) religious affiliation question in the 2001 Census produced the figures in Table 1.1.

Eastborough, like Northcity, is a locality where poverty and deprivation are widespread. Regeneration schemes in surrounding areas have brought changes to the economy and brought new employment opportunities to the area. Nonetheless, the borough remains close to the bottom of the league table of districts on the government's index of multiple deprivation in 2000, and both wards served by the school where we worked are in the most deprived 5 per cent in England. Ethnic diversity is probably unparalleled elsewhere in Britain. The majority of the borough's

Table 1.1: Religious affiliation in the research neighbourhood in Northcity

Ward	Christian (%)	Hindu (%)	Muslim (%)	Sikh (%)	No religion or religion not stated (%)
A	50	5	26	0.3	18
B	54	11	10	0.2	24

Note: Numbers may not add up to 100 per cent due to rounding and the omission of some very small minority categories.

Table 1.2: Religious affiliation in the research neighbourhood in Eastborough

Ward	Christian (%)	Hindu (%)	Muslim (%)	Sikh (%)	No religion or religion not stated (%)
A	21	14	47	5	12
B	47	4	25	0.4	20

Note: Numbers may not add up to 100 per cent due to rounding and the omission of some very small minority categories.

population is from ethnic minorities and the trends are even more pronounced in the catchment area for the school. The local population includes long settled ethnic minority groups originating from the Caribbean and South Asia and groups of more recent migrants and refugees from almost every continent have added to the mix.

In the wards surrounding the school the (voluntary) religious affiliation question in the 2001 Census produced the figures in Table 1.2.

Schools

The two schools in Northcity are church based. One of these schools, referred to as School 1, is a voluntary-controlled Anglican school. The other school, referred to as School 3, is a voluntary-aided Roman Catholic school. Due to the closure of the nearby local Catholic church, School 3 also acts as a place of worship for local parishioners, who attend services during children's school assemblies. The school in Eastborough (School 2), unlike those in Northcity, is a local authority school not attached to a religious institution and has a large majority of children from ethnic minority backgrounds among whom, in terms of religion, Muslims are most numerous. Among the respondents in this school who defined themselves as Christians, all except two were black, from African or Caribbean heritage family backgrounds.

Limitations and ethics

This study is small in scale and is not statistically representative of children in the UK, or even of those living in multi-ethnic neighbourhoods. Our sample by no means covers children from the wide range of religious backgrounds in the UK (for example no Jewish children were involved), or a representative range of schools in terms of religious/secular ethos or diversity of intake. This said, all three schools have children from diverse ethnic and religious backgrounds. Given the deprived inner city locations in which we worked, our sample is probably skewed towards children from less affluent homes, although we have not collected systematic data about family income and social class, variables which are likely to produce variation in patterns of religious observance in all the major religious affiliation groups. Thus, it is important to bear in mind that the findings are likely to be valid only for children living in the particular local contexts we studied and for the specific religious and ethnic diversity mixes these represented. The choice of schools is likely to mean the children have a relatively high awareness of other religions, and probably over-represent observant religious families of various faiths. However, this high salience of religion and range of diversity was crucial to our research, enabling the research team to explore and examine a variety of issues and perspectives of children's views on religion and the role that it plays in their and/or others' lives. It provides a good base from which to begin to address the gap of knowledge in this area.

Access to children involved a series of school visits by members of a research team, who were diverse in their gender, ethnic and religious backgrounds. One was a white male and a practising Christian. He was already known through community, church and family connections in two of the schools, and therefore already recognised by some of the children. The second member, who only worked in the London school, was female, Muslim and of Bangladeshi background and routinely wore Islamic style clothing. The first two members of the team did not attempt to disguise their religious commitments and talked openly with the children about them when asked, while the ethnicity of the third team member (perceived by the children as something other than white 'English') provoked curiosity and many questions about the religion she might be affiliated to, and was the starting point for a number of discussions about ethnic and religious identity. In each school all the researchers undertook interviews with a diverse range of children in terms of gender and religious background. In School 3 fieldwork included an extended presence of two researchers for three days a week over the final half-term of the school year.

In each school a letter was sent home to parents explaining the project and asking for permission for children to take part. In one case the school insisted that parents responded to opt their children *into* the research with the result that over a third of the eligible children could not be approached. In the other two schools the consent letter merely gave parents the opportunity to opt their children *out* and in these two schools only one child was withdrawn. More important was securing the children's own informed consent. All children we met were told several times, in groups and individually, in a written leaflet as well as face to face, that the decision to take part or answer specific questions was theirs. They were also assured repeatedly that individual names and the name of the school would not appear in any published reports and were invited to choose an alias which we would use when referring to individuals. We assured them that everything they told us in interviews would remain strictly confidential to the research team, with the one exception that we might ask their permission to talk with school staff about anything they told us that concerned us about their personal welfare or safety. In the event only one such issue came up and in this case pastoral staff of the school were already aware and taking appropriate action. Hardly any children opted not to take part in the research, which given the power relationships and group dynamics of the classroom would have been quite difficult, although a small number of individuals preferred not to take part in a tape-recorded interview and in one school we were unable to schedule enough time to complete interviews with all the children who were willing. Rather more children did not complete or hand back the diary they were given, and there were numerous occasions when interviewees declined to answer particular questions. In School 3 the children helped us input and begin the analysis of some of the data from the classroom survey. In all the schools we showed appreciation to the whole group by a thank you letter and a small party meal. Those who completed the diary exercise were also rewarded with a small gift.

Research tools

The main research method used to collect and analyse information was semi-structured and topic-led interviews, and usually involved one researcher and two children. There were, however, some one-to-one interviews, and we interviewed several children more than once in different pairs, depending on the situation and preferences of children in the study. Pairings were selected by the children themselves, largely on the basis of friendship. The result of this was that, with very few exceptions, couples were of the same gender, and many were from the same ethnic and/or religious background. Interviews, where possible, were in a quiet place, though researchers were flexible to the arrangements and facilities provided by the schools that participated in the study. Interviews were tape-recorded and transcribed more or less verbatim, and thematic analysis was carried out with the help of a qualitative data analysis package ANSWR 6.0.

Overall, the research project used an eclectic range of classroom exercises and research tools. These included asking children to list children they spent time with in and out of school, and placing names of the significant people in their lives on a diagram in concentric circles by level of importance. We also got them to draw pictures of favourite foods and food places, and played a game sorting foods into different orders depending on whether they liked, disliked, ate them during special occasions or would never eat certain foods. We also used a written survey in the classroom, out-of-school diaries, observations in the classroom and playground, and group discussions. Although we used these exercises and methods to collect data, they also served to build a rapport and develop familiarity between the children and the researchers before the interviews. The records from these activities were also used from time to time as stimulus materials for conversations in the in-depth interviews. Materials which give further details of our methodologies and fieldwork practices, including questionnaires and consent and confidentiality procedures, together with samples of completed diaries and worksheets, statistics from our classroom survey and our network analysis are available on request. Also, they are available on the internet (accessible at http://mysite.wanadoo-members.co.uk/friendsfoodfaith/fffindex.htm).

The research tools were piloted in one of the Northcity schools. In consequence, we made some minor adjustments to some of the instruments and to the letter asking for parental consent. The main change was the researchers' decision to take a less directive and less structured approach in the interviews, and to leave prompting children about faith and religion towards the end of interviews unless these were brought up by the children themselves. However, we also decided to keep a topically structured interview schedule at hand, in order to use the approach which worked best with the children being interviewed. In practice, the interviewers allowed themselves a lot of flexibility in the conversation with children. In some cases the children's contributions were very free flowing and they were allowed to talk to the interviewer and often with the other child present about the topics which interested them. Interviewers tended to respond with open-ended questions that allowed the children to develop what they were saying on a particular theme, and only brought the topic back to a new part of the interview schedule when it was clear that conversation on a topic was exhausted. In other cases children were less forthcoming in their replies and the interviewer might spend more time asking questions or use a child's already completed questionnaire or worksheet to get them talking. It was also evident as the fieldwork in each school progressed that children became more familiar with the researchers, more aware of our interest in particular topics and talked to classmates about completed interviews. Furthermore, as we learned more about some new and interesting themes, the content of the conversations with children and topics we asked about also developed. While we are aware that this approach can be criticised for lack of standardisation, and for introducing the risk of making unwarranted assumptions about what was significant to particular categories of children, it did seem the most effective and appropriate way to explore the children's own perspectives.

Our intention here is, as far as possible, to allow the children's own voices to be heard, and we rely heavily on the analysis of the interview transcripts while the other data collected is sometimes used to provide background insights. However, readers will need to be aware, as we are, that as researchers we have made selections and

Table 1.3: Number of data items for each research exercise by school

	School 1 Northcity	School 2 Eastborough	School 3 Northcity	Total
Number of children involved	32	50	33	115
Classroom survey	32	46	26	104*
Friends network worksheet	32	46	24	102
Food worksheet	31	46	24	101
Diaries	24	28	8	60
Transcribed taped interviews (individuals)	2	2	4	8
Transcribed taped interviews (pairs)	12	14	17	43
Transcribed taped group interviews			4	4
Ethnographic documents etc.	Some photos of class sessions	Set of poems written by pupils of school	Autobio-graphies in PowerPoint format	
		Some photos of class sessions	Best day of my life essays	
			Photos of locality, school and various activities in playground and in class	
Observation field notes	Some about classroom sessions		Extensive on classroom and playground life	

* Only 102 were complete enough for analysis.

interpretations of the data, and that interviews were conversations between particular adults and children in the context and power dynamics of school. In other contexts, for example conversations between children outside school or interviews in the home, different perspectives may well have emerged.

Details of children's involvement in the range of research and class exercises carried out for this study are given in Table 1.3.

Children participating in the study

Over 100 children across the three schools were involved in the research study. This number varied between sessions as some children were away from school or class and some children chose to participate in class exercises but not in the interviews. Here we give basic information collected from the classroom survey to get an overview of the participants. Because different children participated in the research at a variety of different levels, and the in-depth interviews took place mostly in pairs (with some double appearances), we do not have a simple base figure (an n for the total interview sample) against which we can make consistent quantitative statements. Therefore we will avoid using percentages or precise proportions when reporting on trends in the interview data, and even when mentioning numbers of children sharing particular views or experiences these will be expressed in very approximate terms.

Table 1.4 shows that of 102 children who handed in completed surveys, 44 per cent were girls and 56 per cent were boys. This varied slightly across the three different schools. Because in year 6 of School 3 there were no Muslim girls and only one Hindu girl, we interviewed volunteers from year five, who did not participate in the

Table 1.4: Participants in classroom survey by gender and school

			Boys	Girls	Total
102 children from the three schools	School 1	Number	13	19	32
		%	41	60	100
Source: Rapid Survey Data, 2003/4	School 2	Number	19	27	46
		%	41	59	100
	School 3	Number	13	11	24
		%	54	46	100
	Total	Number	45	57	102
		%	44	56	100

other class exercises. These six girls were suggested and asked to take part by their class teacher following a staffroom discussion with the researchers about the characteristics of children who would help balance the sample in terms of gender, religion and ethnicity.

The majority of children taking part in the classroom survey exercise reported their family or self as belonging to a religion. The actual question and categories offered were:

Do you/your family belong to any religion(s)?

No religion ☐
Christian ☐
Muslim ☐
Hindu ☐
Sikh ☐
Jewish ☐
Other Religion _____

Details of our the analysis can be found in Table 1.5.

Under the 'other religion' category, one child had specified 'Pagan', one had ticked both Hindu and Sikh, one 'Combination Christian Sikh Hindu'. Included under Christian are two who had written 'Catholic', one 'Roman Catholic' and one 'Iris Catholic' (sic).

Table 1.5: Participants in classroom survey by family religious affiliation

Family or self belong to any religion(s)?		No religion	Christian	Muslim	Hindu	Sikh	Other religion	Total
School 1	Number	8	12	6	3	1	2	32
	% within school	25	38	19	9	3	6	100
School 2	Number	–	11	27	5	3	–	46
	% within school	–	24	59	11	7	–	100
School 3	Number	–	13	8	2	–	1	24
	% within school	–	54	33	8	–	4	100
Total	Number	8	36	41	10	4	3	102
	%	8	35	40	10	4	3	100

For the reasons we set out later, it is not possible to give a precise account of the ethnicity of all these children and its relation to their religion. But, based on information given to us by children taking part in interviews, we can paint the following picture with some confidence that it captures the salient facts. Throughout the project all the Hindus and Sikhs interviewed had family origins in India, though some families had a history involving residence in East Africa. Most of the Hindus regarded Gujerati as their mother tongue and the Sikhs all spoke Punjabi at home. The majority of Muslims in Schools 1 and 3 were also from Gujerati speaking families of Indian heritage. In these two schools we interviewed one from a Pakistani and one from a Bangladeshi heritage. In School 2 in Eastborough there was more diversity among the Muslim children although not every child talked about their ethnic or national heritage. The largest groups for whom we have information were of Bangladeshi and Pakistani heritage but there were also Gujeratis and one each from Somali and South African families. In School 1 all the children who claimed no religion were white, as were all the Christians and the sole pagan. Among the Christians in this school one or two children we talked to indicated they considered themselves to be Roman Catholic, and one talked of attending an independent church, while the rest identified at least passively with the local Anglican parish. In School 2 only a couple of the Christian children were white, and the rest came from African or Caribbean heritage families, while, of those we interviewed, five attended a Roman Catholic church, one an Anglican church and one a church which was most probably majority black and Pentecostal (although he did not use those labels). In School 3 all the Christian children in the year six group were white and considered themselves Catholic bar one who attended an Anglican church. However, we also interviewed two children from year five who were both of African heritage and worshipped at an Evangelical and Mormon church respectively.

2. Research findings 1: children's believing and belonging – a framework for analysis

In this first section of findings we examine the data from the interviews with children which can be used to address questions about religious identity and belonging, and their accounts and perspectives about various kinds of believing or not believing. From this we propose a framework for analysis which will help us interpret the variation and complexity in the relationships between children and religion.

Religious affiliation and identity

It is important initially to explain why we use the terms 'believing' and 'belonging' in the title of this report, and what we are trying to convey by this. This explanation is especially important as it will become apparent that in only a minority of the data presented in this report, and indeed in the corpus of data from the interviews, do children talk explicitly about the content of their religious belief or spiritual experiences. Nor, for that matter, in the material presented here do the children talk explicitly about belonging and the emotional importance of their religious affiliation. The phrase derives from the work of Grace Davie (1994) whose book used the subtitle *Believing without Belonging* to sum up the religious mood of mainstream English culture. In the following decade the phrase has become widely used in popular versions of sociology of religion, while academics have explored the complexities of religious identity and religious and ethnic diversity in more detail (for further details see Smith 2004). By using this phrase we do not wish to imply that children involved in our research belonged in any formal sense to religious institutions, or believed in any formal body of religious doctrine. The nature and indeed the existence of religions and religious groups, or such concepts as 'faith communities' or 'traditions' is problematic, yet we needed to use everyday language including such terms when talking to the children. In doing so we found that all the children involved understood the terms religion and faith, and that most of them saw themselves as belonging to a religion. Many were involved in the practices of religion and some talked about believing in the divine in ways they had been taught, or had come to believe by personal exploration. For many of the children in our research the most important thing about religion was that they were living in a milieu where the observance of religion was commonplace and where believing in and belonging to a religion was taken as the norm. At the end of this section, after presenting some of the data, we will develop in more detail a framework which we hope will clarify various aspects of the place of religion in children's lives.

The children in our sample, with few exceptions, were willing to identify themselves as affiliated to a religion. Of 102 children who completed our classroom survey 40 per cent identified themselves and their family as Muslim, 35 per cent as Christian, 10 per cent as Hindu, 4 per cent as Sikh, 3 per cent as other or some mixture and 8 per cent as of no religion. It is hard to assess how far these high levels of religious identification were influenced by the research being introduced as 'Friends, Food and Faith', but it seems plausible that this focus gave religion an unusual salience in the conversations. The location of research in two 'church' schools may also have biased findings in this direction, but it is interesting that it was only in a Church of England school that any children claimed to be of no religion, and that every pupil in a local education authority school identified with a religion. It also seems likely that figures would be lower in other more affluent and less diverse locations than the multi-ethnic inner urban neighbourhoods in which the project worked.

Religion, often linked with ethnicity, featured in some children's discussion of their identity and differences between them and others. However, it was by no means the only or the most important variable mentioned, since gender and age group played a large part in shaping friendship networks before religion or ethnicity came into play.

Because of the complex interrelationship between ethnicity and religious belonging and believing, it has proved extremely difficult to talk about individual children in terms of a simple set of categories representing religious affiliation. It is not easy from the transcripts to untangle whether children talked about religion or ethnicity, as often they did not make clear distinctions, although they were usually able to do so when prompted by the interviewers. For example, there were several references to children 'speaking Muslim', and language as well as lifestyle differences related to religion were important . We also recognised widespread working assumptions among both children and adults that all white people are Christian, and only Asian people are Hindu or Muslim.

We did not ask children an 'ethnicity' question in our rapid classroom survey because we did not believe it was possible to reduce a complex set of identity process to a single, multiple choice question. However, in the in-depth interviews, we often discussed the issues of ethnicity and contacts with the culture and country of the family's origins. Indeed, an analysis of the data around ethnic identity, and inter-community relationship issues as they were discussed by the children, could offer material for a report in its own right. We also heard quite a lot of conversation by children and staff which referred to children in terms of ethnic categories, and did not make it our business to challenge or question them about this. There are huge complexities in assigning individuals to an ethnic category, whether this is done by self-report or by others, and dangers in making assumptions about the existence or unity of 'ethnic groups'. However, there are strong correlations between national heritage and religious identity both for children in our sample and in wider society. Furthermore, in the case of some religions there are adherents from a wide variety of ethnic or national heritages, and in some cases the meaning and practices of the religion may vary along cultural or ethnic lines. In spite of the advice of some colleagues, we have resisted the temptation to assign all children to a clearly defined set of ethnic categories or to present statistics breaking down our sample by ethnic categories. Yet because it is impossible to ignore the relationships between religious and ethnic identity, there are occasions in this report where (in view of the context) we point them out, or label children with a broad ethnic category (such as black or white) alongside a religious one. While we recognise that this is unsatisfactory in terms of sociological rigour, and depends upon researchers' perceptions and judgements, at some points a comment about a child's ethnicity seems helpful. However, we have been sparing in our use of ethnic labels, and as far as possible religious affiliation is the key variable that is used.

On the basis of our data and other research literature we cannot assume any of the major 'religions' is a unified institution with an uncontested body of belief and practice. However, we had to employ a straightforward set of religious identity categories for the practical purposes of coding and labelling the sources of quotations used in the text. We need, however, to beware of the assumption that any child who uses or is described by one of these religious affiliation labels, belongs, weakly or strongly, to an actual community of faith, or personally has a faith, beliefs or practices of spirituality associated with a religion. The salience and significance of religious identities varies both across and within these groups of children labelled by religion.

All the Muslim children we talked to accepted and affirmed their identity as Muslims and for a large number of them the religious dimension of their identity appeared paramount and a matter of pride. At least three or four interviews began rather like this, before the interviewer could say a word: 'My name it is J... and I live in (street) in this town ... I'm a Muslim and my religion is Islam. I go to mosque every day, we have five prayers a day' (Muslim boy, School 3).

In contrast, none of the Hindu or Christian children, who equally knew that we were interested in finding out about religion, began to talk about religion unprompted. However, among the Muslim children there are variations in the extent of Islamic practices and definitions of Islamic identity. For example, two highly observant Muslim girls discussed (with a female Muslim interviewer who was herself wearing a headscarf) markers of a 'proper' Muslim female, one speaking thus:

> Interviewer: What do you like about them [friends]?
> They wear scarf like me. And they play cricket and rounders and basketball.
> Interviewer: So does it make a difference whether someone wears a scarf or not to be your friend?
> Yeah.
> Interviewer: Why?
> Because when some people don't wear scarves they don't really act like a Muslim.
> *(Muslim girl, School 2)*

The category Hindu is also hard to define. We discovered that some children in this category participate in Christian activities including Sunday mass attendance, as well as in Hindu rituals at home and temple. Hindu children recognised that there were often variations in the extent of religious practice between and within families, and often suggested the older generation was more religious than they were. One boy, for example, told us his grandmother was always 'acting like a priest'. The term Sikh covers only a handful of children in our sample but again is problematic. At least one child told us her family took part in worship both at the Gurudwara and a local Hindu temple. Another Sikh boy, who gave a detailed account of the identity markers of the Sikh Khalsa (the uncut hair, comb, bangle, dagger and underpants, often referred to as the 5 Ks), was explicitly aware of the historical links between the religions, telling us that Guru Nanak was actually a Hindu, and mentioning that Sikhs celebrate Diwali.

For individual children of Indian heritage religious identity, especially at the family level, can be even more complicated. For example a girl who defined herself as a Hindu said:

> I don't go to Hindu classes, just like once in a week I go to a Gurudwara. And I have been to church with my auntie ... sometimes I go temple, and Gurudwara with my other auntie.

Interviewer: So your auntie is Sikh?
Yeah. And my other auntie, the one [whose conversion] I talked to you about that's Christian, when I go to her house ... I go to the church with her on Sundays.
(Hindu girl, School 2)

The term 'Christian' is even more difficult to define with any consistency. For children from a white British (or Irish) family background it is a default term, which is often applied to them by Muslim or Hindu children, by the school authorities and sometimes by themselves, regardless of whether they or their families belong to, or attend a church, or believe anything that is recognisably Christian doctrine.

The children in who said they were of 'no religion' were all white and attended School 1. Yet even here there was some ambiguity, as some who had first said they had 'no religion' then said they believed the basic Christian teachings about God and Jesus and even that they attended church activities.

I believe in all the Christian things, but I don't really go to church or nothing. I pray ... I pray at school and everything, I don't like pray of my free will ... I used to go to Brownies when I was about seven, and I go to this thing in St ... church ... I go to a club ... it's like when you learn about God and things in a fun way.
(girl, 'no religion', School 1)

In contrast, among the black (African or Caribbean heritage) children in our sample (apart from two Muslims with African family backgrounds), *all* called themselves Christians (about 10 in the classroom survey), and all seven who were interviewed told us they were involved with their families in *active* membership of a church. This correlation between ethnicity and high levels of Christian religious practice is hardly a surprise to anyone familiar with church life in inner city areas or in the light of research findings such as the fourth Policy Studies Institute survey (Modood and others 1997). Like the Hindu children, observant Christians sometimes pointed out that there were generational differences in the strength of religious practice; in many cases it was the grandmother who was the most pious member of the family.

In the light of this complexity we have concluded that it is not possible to use a single, simple and consistent term to identify those children who live within a culture corresponding to what British education law calls 'of a broadly or mainly Christian character'. Therefore, we apply the categories flexibly and with contextual variation, for example when talking about first communion or serving at mass it makes sense to label a child as 'Catholic' rather than 'Christian'. Also there are times when the ethnicity of a child is significant for understanding the context, and where terms such as 'white Christian' or 'black Catholic' are employed. The term 'nominal Christian' is sometimes used as a shorthand way of referring to children who may express a religious affiliation, and profess some beliefs they regard as Christian, but who have little or no meaningful involvement in any organised religious activity outside school.

Social observance of religion

Children in the project tended to talk about religion and faith, both their own (if they had one) and of others, in two distinct but often overlapping ways. On the one hand, there were conversations about religion which were essentially objective and social, including discussion of religious institutions, shared religious practices, and stories, beliefs and values which had been transmitted to them by adults. On the other hand (somewhat less often), children also talked about personal belief, ritual practices and spirituality with which they engaged as social actors in their own right, that often drew on inherited religious traditions, but which also had a more subjective and creative element.

For many, the social practice of religion may be largely a matter of obligation arising from belonging to a family that was actively involved in a community of faith. Children often referred to activities which they were either expected to do, or 'not allowed' to do according to the teachings of their religion. They also talked about being taken, or being sent to, churches, temples, Gurudwaras and mosques to take part in rituals, ceremonies or acts of worship, or to attend religious instruction or classes in language and culture. It is clear that some children would prefer to be doing other things than religion on these occasions, perhaps naturally enough in a culture which tends to regard mainstream school as 'work' and the rest of life as 'leisure'. There are examples in the transcripts of a Hindu boy who appears to resent a parental requirement for him to attend temple, and of a Catholic girl who told us:

> Sundays, it's the most boring day of the week.
> Interviewer: Why is it boring?
> I go church ... the priest go on ... we don't even know what he's talking about most of the time.
> *(Christian girl, School 2)*

Among Muslims, whose daily schedules often involved several hours of religious activity, there were some who made envious comparisons with the freer lives of classmates:

Interviewer: If you had your own choice ... completely had your own freedom what would you do after school?

Boy 1: Play out ...

Boy 2: It's OK for Christians ...

Interviewer: You think it's okay for Christians do you?

Boy 1: They can play outside ...

(Two Muslim boys, School 3)

Some non-Muslim children clearly believed that Muslim children were compelled to practise their religion in a way which contrasted, at least in degree, with their own experience:

Girl 1: I think theirs is more strict and it's more about this is your religion and it is like ... for us you can come to church if you want ... but for them it is you *will* go ...

Girl 2: In Muslim ... in mosque I keep forgetting what it is called ... people get whipped if they are not at mosque ... and they get whipped ... if they turn up late ...

(Christian girl and Hindu girl, School 3)

It is hard to judge whether they had formed this understanding on the basis of a common stereotype (which as we shall see later is far from the whole truth), or as a result of conversations they had had with schoolmates.

On the other hand, there were many children who reported they not only accepted the regular practice of their religion as a duty, but enjoyed attending activities at mosque, church or temple and showed pride in achievements such as keeping fasts or memorising scripture. A number of children were choosing or attempting to attend religious activities despite parental indifference, sometimes with the support of another adult relative or sometimes on their own. For example:

Girl 1: I've a Bible in my room. My mum won't take me to church though – I want to go to church

Interviewer: You want to go to church?

Girl 2: I'm allowed to go when ... I go down to my nan's in [city of N. England] and she'll take me to church. She doesn't really believe in God but she knows I do, so she'll take me to church sometimes if she's got time, but my mum won't. She says she's got too much work to do.

(Two Christian girls, School 1)

Personal faith and spirituality

Before looking at children's accounts on this theme, it is important to point out that the very idea of people holding an individual faith or practising personal regimes of spirituality is shaped differently in different cultures. Individualism is particularly strong in late modern, western Christian influenced culture, and although most of the major religious traditions, including some streams of Islam, recognise personal devotion, other religions may be essentially more corporate and ritualistic in their approach. Muslim children in particular tended to talk about their religion in terms of social practice, received teachings and morality and ethics rather than as personal devotion or belief.

The children who indicated they had a personal faith ranged from those who accepted the religious tradition they had been taught, to the one or two individuals who had clearly made a personal commitment to a faith. For example, a Christian girl at School 3 (from a black African background) had a faith which sealed her belonging to the family's evangelical church.

> But [my sister and I] just got saved ... And then we had to get baptised ...
> Interviewer: How would you explain to me what getting saved is?
> When you ... have given your life to Jesus ... and you listen to him ... And you try to do all the good deeds ... But you try to listen to the Bible ... And do what it says in the Bible.

It was evident from the interviews that some children had an everyday awareness of the presence of the divine, and that their believing took precedence over their social practice of religion. Our only pagan respondent told us in a quite straightforward way that 'the Goddess talks to me' and his imaginary friend (who had been listed on his network diagram and already discussed in the interview) also takes part in these spiritual conversations. A number of children from Christian and Hindu backgrounds included God on their network diagrams of important other people in their lives as in the example below 'I've put as closest God ... because He is everywhere ... [then] my mum, my dog, my baby sister' (Christian boy, School 2).

Many children talked about prayer or meditation as a personal spiritual practice, covering such situations as coping with school work and needing God's help in tests and exams. One girl spoke of seeking divine help when sad:

> I'm glad that God is in my life because like say I'm a bit down in the dumps, I'm a bit sad, I can always pray and talk to God ... God's always

there for you as well and that's something to hold on to – say if you're like ill or something like that.
(Christian girl, School 3)

In a similar way, one Christian boy spoke of praying daily that he would be helped to keep out of trouble at school, another of prayer about controlling his own difficult behaviour, and a Sikh boy of how meditating on the name of his God was an effective help for getting good marks in a mental maths test.

On the other hand, a few children who did express a strong religious affiliation, and regularly attended worship said that in fact they were not very religious or did not pray very often:

> Hindu girl: Half of me is really into religion like I do loads of things, doing things in the community. Half of me I go to any place of worship like ... I just go cos I like going ... And sometimes when I have to go to religious festivals sometimes if I don't go ... that's what I mean by half religion, if I don't feel religious I don't go.
> Interviewer: And what about you F...?
> Christian girl: I am half of it cos I like going to church and going on things I like, going on like parish trips and everything but I'm not like I pray everyday like that and I won't do everything like pray after lunch unless it's at school cos we have to do that, but I'm not like I will do everything.
> *(School 3)*

Children frequently talked about their beliefs about what happens to people after death. Muslim children tended to talk to us about issues of God's justice and judgement on evil, with a strong emphasis on eternal reward or punishment:

> Girl 1: Um you should follow the rule of what Allah has given us and what he says because he's made us and the world. And my Gran said that you have to do wuzu and namaz five times a day. And when it's the end of the world like its gonna effect you, there's gonna be a place where you have to go to, heaven or hell.
> Girl 2: Yeah that's the most important thing.
> *(Two Muslim girls, School 2)*

A few of the Christian children also expressed some concern with sin and its consequences, but none of them put much emphasis on ideas of retribution, talking rather about forgiveness or even salvation. In discussions of the afterlife some children exercised a degree of imaginative speculation. One pair of nominally

Christian girls were sure there must be a special 'catty heaven' for their pets, and speculated about the nature of heaven thus:

> Girl 1: What I thought when I was a bit younger ... when I was six I really did think that there were two sorts ... There was all the same heaven ... but when women died ... they got all these designer wings, and long fantasy robes.
> Girl 2: Fingernails.
> Girl 1: And sunset glasses ... and they were all given a little pet hamster which was in a little black thing ... with a little halo.
> Girl 2: And men get massive widescreen TVs with the football always on.
> Girl 1: And I think it all the grown-ups who died who are between 25 and 30 they have to go back to school, all the teachers who died had to go back to school.
> Interviewer: It sounds like hell rather.
> Girl 1: Heaven! Heaven for us.
> Girl 2: But children who died they don't have to go to school ...
> Girl 1: They got to do anything they wanted.
> Girl 2: Old people who died they didn't have to go to school ... if my mum died ... she wouldn't, she is a teacher but obviously there are exceptions ... Made for her ... Because she is nice.
> *(Two Christian girls, School 1)*

An analytic framework and typology

In the light of this we present a framework for analysis of our data. Because we embarked on this research with an open approach to discovering children's perspectives on religion rather than from a fixed theoretical perspective, we have tried and tested a number of alternative ways to interpret the children's accounts of their experiences. This is only one of many possible ways of telling the story of the project, but we believe it is a very useful one as we think it would be recognisable by the children we talked to, while at the same time it can be mapped on to the understandings and theories we have drawn from our reading of the various sociologies of religion, ethnicity, institutions and childhood.

Our first step was to try to reduce the complexity of children's accounts of religion to three dimensions, which are conceptually independent but in practice may be intricately interwoven.

1. Affiliation, identity and belonging covers the way a person is labelled by self and/or others as a member of a religion, the affective feelings of identification with a religious tradition, and willingness or obligation to participate in the rituals and activities associated with that tradition. This dimension is complex and hard to define, because religious categories may have permeable boundaries and subdivisions. Furthermore, there may be strong correlations between religion and ethnicity, whether the categories used for each are defined by the subject or ascribed externally. Our understanding of the concept of identity, derived from social theory and the literature in this field and reinforced by our analysis of the data, does not allow us to ascribe a single essential identity either to individuals or groups. Rather, identity processes may be fluid, with multiple identities which may be context dependent, or have variable salience at different moments. It is also important in this approach to understand identities as being constructed largely in the light of the perceptions of other groups. Thus, for example, a person identifying as a Christian may mean something very different if the context is one where 'Muslims' have already been recognised as significant others, compared with a situation in which Muslims are not present in significant enough numbers to be noticed.

2. Social observance of religion is the practice of the structured learning, rituals, ceremonies and festivals associated with a religion either in public or within the family. Observance may by low or high, but may also vary over time, and be differentiated according to the gender, age, status and defined roles of particular individuals.

3. Personal faith, belief and spirituality cover the elements of the religious which are located in the mind (or soul) of the individual – beliefs, thoughts, emotions and practices such as private prayer and meditation.

In consequence of these distinctions 'Religion' is generally used in this report to denote the social, or institutional aspects of human relationships with the divine (mainly as in 2 above). 'Faith' in contrast is used in this report as a more personal and individual property. Readers will no doubt be aware of the common use of terms like 'the world faiths', 'faith communities', 'faith-based organisations', the 'world faiths' and 'inter-faith dialogue'. To avoid confusion we will avoid such usage wherever possible except, of course, in quotations.

We have found it helpful to develop a typology which helps us understand how different types of children relate to these three dimensions. As a series of five 'ideal types' this scheme is not meant to represent either a simple set of discrete categories into which each individual case can unambiguously fit, nor even a one-dimensional

Table 2.1: Our typology

Type	Characteristics	In the project sample members of this type are most likely to be:
1. Highly observant		
Religious identity very significant High level of social practice Medium or high level of belief and spirituality	Such children describe their lives as significantly shaped by their religion. They are likely to be heavily involved in the practices and institutions of their religion and quite strongly committed to the beliefs and values they have been taught.	Muslims - especially the 'mosque boys' in Northcity, and some religious (headscarf wearing) girls in Eastborough Also evangelical or sectarian Christians - the few in our sample were from black African backgrounds
2. Observant		
Religious identity significant Medium level of social practice Medium or low level of belief and spirituality	Such children describe religious observance as playing a compulsory, significant and regular part in their lives. They usually accept its teachings and practices although they may find some or all of it boring or an imposition.	Some Muslims Most of the Sikhs and Hindus Churchgoing Christians (most of the black children)
3. Occasionally participating		
Religious identity may be significant Low (but may desire higher) level of social practice Medium level of belief and spirituality	Such children do not get taken or sent to religious activities by their adults except on rare special occasions, and are unlikely to be well instructed in their religion. They do identify with the religion, may attend voluntarily, without adults, and enjoy benefits such as fun clubs, festivals, feasts and presents.	White nominal Christians Some Hindus ... who may also attend activities of other religions

Table 2.1: Our typology (cont'd)

Type	Characteristics	In the project sample members of this type are most likely to be:
4. Implicit individual faith		
Religious identity may, but need not, be significant High, medium or low level of social practice High level of belief and spirituality	These children concentrate on religion as the realm of the supernatural and talk about personal spirituality, drawing on faith as a resource through prayer, meditation, rituals etc. They may attend or belong to religious institutions and express a religious affiliation, but these are not essential to their understanding of faith.	Some churchgoing and nominal Christians, a pagan, at least one Sikh, and two Muslim girls whose most significant experience of religion took place in a vernacular tradition of Islam found in Gujerat
5. Not religious		
Religious identity not significant Low social practice Low level of belief and spirituality	Such children have little interest in or understanding of religion, or experience of it outside of school, and may question or mock those who are religious.	All were white children in School 1 in Northcity

continuum on which they can be placed. However, we did find children whose relation to religion was meaningful in terms of this typology, and some broad trends which suggest how other variables might correlate with these types. It should be noted that individuals from every possible religious background might be found in any of the five main categories of this typology, any associations or correlations between particular religions and types such as those suggested in the third column in Table 2.1 are purely an empirical matter, which in this limited research project should be taken as merely indicative, rather than as established findings.

The key findings of our preliminary exploration of children's conversations about religious identity, practice and personal faith, are that:

- Children's patterns of religious observance were not strictly and simply related to religious affiliation or being labelled as an adherent of one of the 'world religions'. Rather, they emerged in the context of a complex pattern of identity and belonging which might involve, among other things, kinship, ethnicity, age and gender.

- Within each of the various religious affiliation groups there were children with different levels and patterns of both the social observance of their religion, and personal commitment to and understanding of faith. Within our sample there was a tendency for the Muslim children to be at the more observant end of the spectrum and white children to be at the least observant end.

3. Research findings 2: believing and belonging in school

In this section we consider children's accounts of their lives within schools marked by ethnic and religious diversity and the part this plays within their formal and informal activities. We move on to looking at the nature of friendship and social circles formed or maintained within the primary school, and how religion plays a part in shaping children's social networks.

Diversity in school

The primary schools in which the research took place were almost certainly some of the few institutions in the neighbourhood where people from various ethnic and religious backgrounds mixed on an extended day-to-day basis. We heard that some children positively enjoyed the mixture of people and cultures in their schools, that learning about other religions was fun, and was helped by having different religions represented in school.

> Well, I definitely prefer a mixed school because ... I get on with loads and loads of different people and I don't care what religion they are ... I mean [if it was only Christians] it would be boring because you wouldn't be allowed to ... I mean you wouldn't be learning about Islam, Hindu or Sikh religion in RE, you'd just be learning about Christians and going on about reading the Bible and yab yab yab. I mean it is good fun to learn about other religions.
>
> *(Christian girl, School 1)*

Many children of various religious affiliations spoke in a similar positive way about diversity as they covered a range of topics in the interviews:

Interviewer: Did you think of going to a Muslim school?

No ... I really like a mixed school not a Muslim one, because I really like to know about all different other people and the way they live and their religions and all that.
(Muslim girl, School 2)

I would prefer mixed schools because then you know what it is like to be a Christian or a Muslim ... If you want to be a Christian and you don't know what it's like to be a Christian ... you know what it feels like before you be a Christian.
(Sikh girl, School 1)

However, in some children's accounts there were some indications of areas of tension and conflict over religion and religio-ethnic identity. For example, number balance between groups within the school seems to matter, especially to some of the boys from minority religious groups. Two Muslim boys in School 3 felt it was important that there were substantial numbers of Muslims in the secondary school they were going to as a support and friendship group:

Interviewer: Now [the secondary school you are going to] is a Christian school ... a Catholic school
Boy 1: There's a lot of Asians there ... a lot of Muslims ...
Interviewer: Do you think it matters that it is a Christian school ... a Catholic school?
Boy 1: If there were no Muslims there then I wouldn't go ... but there are a lot of Muslims.
Interviewer: Why do you think it is important there are a lot of Muslims there?
Boy 2: If there were only one or two Muslims it is going to be quite boring ... because we only play with Muslims.
(Two Muslim boys, School 3)

Similarly, two Sikh boys in School 2 preferred what they considered as a 'mixed' school because they felt they might be overwhelmed by large numbers of Muslim classmates in schools in their neighbourhood:

I want to go to [a school in a nearby Sikh-dominated neighbourhood] ... because ... I'm not trying to be racist but ... in this area there are so many Muslims ... and on Eid most of them stay at home and there are only five or six people in our class ... and most ... Some people get bullied by them.
(Sikh boy, School 2)

Several white Christian children talked about their experience of moving to schools with different proportions of children from different religions. One who had moved from a majority white school to School 3 said she had soon found it was easy to get on with Muslims and Hindus. A boy who had made a similar change said he 'was a bit edgy in case they would be like really different and they didn't like me', but 'I'm fine with Muslims now'. Another child who had actually moved to Northcity from Eastborough noticed that it was harder to make friends across religions:

> ... all the Muslim kids seem to keep themselves to themselves here.
> Interviewer: Was it like that in London?
> No, we used to always go around together, I mean [my brother] was a strong Christian and all his friends were just going around Muslims, Hindus, Sikhs whatever. I mean one of my best mates in London was Sikh [boy], S...
> Interviewer: And do you think it doesn't happen as much here?
> Yeah, it doesn't happen that much at all. People keep themselves to themselves ... like all the Asian kids stick together really.
> *(White Christian girl, School 1)*

This suggests children can be aware that different group dynamics operate in different local settings, according to the demographic make up of the school and local community and established patterns of inter-group relationships. A tentative explanation which would cast some light on the difference between Northcity and Eastborough schools might run as follows. Children find being in a school where there is religious and ethnic diversity a positive experience. However, if their own identity group is a small minority, they are likely to feel anxious, especially if the category in which they are placed is viewed negatively or excluded by wider society and the dominant group. Thus Muslim children in a school with a majority of Christians (Northcity), or Sikh children in a school where Muslims form a big majority (Eastborough), may feel vulnerable, and need to group together for security. This may be less the case for Christian children in a numerical minority as they remain part of a dominant majority culture at a wider level. Strict observance of a religion may tend to reinforce difference and separation between groups, while in a situation where one religion is numerically dominant differences within that religion may come to the fore. Thus in Northcity Christian children talked more about the varying content of their personal faith, and in Eastborough Muslims talked about the differing strictness of Islamic practice, for example about wearing headscarves.

Faith-based schools

Many children were not very aware of a particular religious ethos in their schools. In the two church schools almost all the children who made a comment, regardless of religious backgrounds, seemed quite relaxed about the unexceptional nature of their school. In the local education authority school (School 2) hardly any comments were made about the (lack of) religious ethos.

> Interviewer: This is a Catholic school – what does that mean to you?
> Never thought about it, we just think of it as our school.
> *(White Roman Catholic girl, School 3)*
>
> Interviewer: It's really a Christian school ... linked to a Christian church ... How you feel about that? Does it make any difference to you?
> Boy 1: Not really ...
> Boy 2: I think a school is a school.
> *(Two Muslim boys, School 1)*

While children may well be indifferent to faith-based schooling, parents may have firmer views. One or two white girls in Northcity hinted that their parents preferred a church primary school, in one case because of the explicit religious ethos and teaching, and in another because their parents would not allow them to go to another local primary school because it was 'full of Muslims'. This comment, which was set in the wider context of a conversation about ethnic difference and conflict in the neighbourhood, suggests that children are aware of and may be influenced by adult views and prejudices. It may also cast light on the local ethnic dynamics in Northcity which, as we see elsewhere in this report, may sometimes lead to a lack of social mixing between the Muslim minority and the wider population.

For children nearing the end of year 6 the question of moving to secondary school was high on the agenda. The interviews suggest children would like to go to the same school as friends from primary school and/or older siblings or kin, but not to a school with a bad reputation for bullying, violence or racial harassment, or the way teachers treat students. Some children, especially Muslims, told us that they would much prefer a single-sex school while some of the white girls strongly preferred a mixed school where there were lots of 'fit lads'.

Most children did not seem to have very strong views about the desirability of 'church' schools, and Sikh or Hindu schools were not available locally. Most Muslim children, however, did have (some limited) options for various forms of Islamic schooling and many said they and their parents had seriously considered them. Some of them argued that it would be good to be in a school where they could learn their own religion, and where they would be free from the pressure to take part in un-Islamic practices. Others thought the Islamic schools they knew of were not well resourced or comfortable places to study. Finally, some children had heard that the regime in such schools was harsh, both in terms of the schoolwork and discipline:

> Interviewer: Your brother goes to this Islamic school ... do you think you will end up going there?
> Yes in a few years ... or the one in Leicester ...
> Interviewer: What you think about Islamic schools – do you think they are a good idea?
> I think they are too strict ... they are stricter, they have got small classes.
> *(Muslim boy, School 1)*

Only a handful of Muslim children were actually anticipating going to an Islamic secondary school or college, while the majority were heading for a neighbourhood high school, either church or secular. In some cases this was because places were hard to obtain or travel arrangements would be inconvenient, as for this girl:

> I'm going [default comprehensive], and um ... I wanted to go to the Islamic girls' school.
> Interviewer: Why did you want to go to an Islamic school?
> Because its girls' school.
> Interviewer: So what happened, how come you're going to [default comprehensive]?
> My dad said you can't go to Islamic girls' school cos that one's quite far and this one's near.
> *(Muslim girl, School 2)*

Assemblies and RE lessons

We tried to explore with the children their perception of the religious ethos of their schools by asking questions about RE lessons, prayers and assemblies. Variations between schools came out in children's descriptions. Some of the differences may reflect the existence or absence of formal connections with the church, although it is possible that other factors, especially the long-term experience of working with a particular number balance between pupils from different religions, may have an influence. Children at the two church schools were familiar with visits from the local vicar or priest and with a Christian content to assembly. In the Catholic school

(School 3) children also commented about prayers at meals and even in the classroom, and about acts of worship such as mass on feast days. In the LEA school (School 2) children indicated that assemblies were less overtly religious.

Most of the issues about assemblies were practical rather than religious ones. Children expressed enjoyment when achievements were recognised and praised, and disliked it when they were told off or given lectures on school rules. Some Muslim boys complained they were usually required to sit alternately in rows with the girls, rather than with their own friends. Sometimes children found assemblies boring, or even painful, as they were required to sit still on a hard floor for long periods.

> Interviewer: What did you think of assembly?
> Quite boring really cos you sit on the rock hard solid floor and your bum hurts.
> *(Christian boy, School 3)*

In all three schools the children told us, and we observed evidence, that RE lessons covered a multi-faith syllabus, which some found interesting and others less so:

> Girl 1: It's interesting cos I learn about different cultures. Not just the same cultures that I know.
> Interviewer: What about you, how do you find doing RE at school?
> Girl 2: I find it boring.
> Interviewer: Boring, ok.
> Girl 2: No but if we go on the trips like, in year 5 we had an RE project about Sikhs, we went to a Sikh Gurudwara and that was fun.
> *(Two Muslim girls, School 2)*

Many children gave accounts of things they had learned about religions other than their own, but often concentrating on issues that fascinated them such as the nature or absence of underwear required when Muslims go on the Haj, rather than on the key themes that the RE syllabus might try to communicate. Several appreciated what they had learned about other religions than their own:

> Our first lesson was about Muslims, then Christianity.
> Interviewer: And what do you think about those lessons?
> It's good ...
> Interviewer: What was good?
> I didn't know about the precepts of Buddhism now I do ... And I didn't know that much about Christianity but now I do ...

> Interviewer: What do you know about Christianity now?
> Some of it is the same ... [as Islam].
> *(Muslim boy, School 2)*

Others, in particular where interviews were in mixed religion pairs, warmed to the topic of religious difference and began to engage with the interviewer in their own inter-faith dialogues as in this case between a Muslim and a pagan:

> Interviewer: What do you think of your friend's religion?
> Muslim boy: I think it's really good ... I would be interested in it ... If I ... I would really like to be that as well ... but I like to be my religion as well ... that is a really good religion ... though I like the way you get to talk to your God ... we don't get to talk to our God ... but we think ... he doesn't talk back to us but we think we are talking to him and he is the only forgiver and the merciful ... that sort of thing and ...
> Interviewer: Now you know this school is Saint ... And it's a Christian church school really ... now how does that fit in with your religion ... for instance you have assemblies and prayers?
> Muslim boy: That is actually fine with me ... I'm just say ... when they say their prayer ... I don't actually say amen ... I do my own prayer ... for my God ... and I do the translating of what they say ...
> Interviewer: What about you ... how you feel about assembly and Christian things?
> Pagan boy: It's all right but some of the songs ... I don't really sing some of the songs ... but some of the [ones I] like I do, some of them which aren't Christian songs. I say my own prayers as I said before ... And I think his religion is quite good ... but I think it is quite difficult as well.
> *(Muslim boy and pagan boy, School 1)*

Generally children from religious minority backgrounds said they appreciated it when their own religion was discussed and they had an opportunity to show off their expert inside knowledge, or where other children were asking about their religion. For example:

> [RE is] ... interesting; we are doing Islam ... I am finding a lot of people are liking it ... when we are supposed to be spending half an hour it goes right through the whole afternoon because people are putting their hands up for questions.
> *(Muslim boy, School 1)*

School policies and practices on religious diversity

However, some children also told us of some patterns of exclusion or lack of religious awareness on the part of their schools. For some Muslim children these became issues of segregation from other children and tension with the school authorities. For example, one Muslim girl complained that a Christian girl in her class had actually handled the Holy Quran without the proper respectful preparation (wudhu).

The schools had a clear policy, which meant that parents could ask for their children to be withdrawn from acts of Christian worship in school. In the Catholic school we found that this option was taken up by most Muslim children, and by at least one evangelical Christian child, who went to another room under the supervision of a Muslim teacher and did some homework or fun activities. Interestingly, almost all the Hindu children took part in worship, even going up to receive a blessing from the priest when mass was celebrated.

School lunches were also an event that tended to mark religious difference. In School 3 grace was said at the start of meals and some of the Muslim children remarked that this was something they were not allowed to take part in. Separate tables for packed lunches, halal, vegetarian and what some children and staff described as 'normal' food tended to reinforce segregation, although this was not absolute, as we encountered Christians who were vegetarian and one Hindu who preferred to eat the halal meals. In fact, most of the Muslim children in School 3 brought a packed lunch which they could be sure was halal.

In Northcity, Muslim children also appeared less likely than others to take part in some extracurricular activities organised by the school such as field studies trips and after-school clubs. For the most part they put the latter down to the time slot after school being required for lessons at mosque, but other factors such as parental caution about mixed gender activities or the programme of activities may also play a part. But it is interesting that in School 2 in Eastborough many Muslim children told us that they did take part in such activities.

One issue which was highly significant to many of the Muslim children in Northcity was that of music and singing in school, although the issue did not arise in a significant way among Muslim children we talked to in Eastborough. Children in Schools 1 and 3 had to take part in singing, although it was felt to be against Islam to sing at all, and doubly so if the lyrics reflected Christian beliefs. Two Muslim girls actually told us of one type of traditional song that was permitted for Muslims and background research suggests a variety of views about music within Islam (Halstead 1994). However, in several local mosques in Northcity, which are led by people of Indian heritage, there is a strong view that music is un-Islamic. In an assembly we observed, which included a singing practice, Christian songs and hymns which were being practised for mass were performed with hardly audible voices and no enthusiasm. Yet when, as a finale, the whole school was invited to sing 'Chitty Chitty Bang Bang' all the children, including most of the Muslims, joined in with great gusto. Muslim children often said that in order to keep out of trouble they would 'mouth' the words of songs. This action, they told us, had been advised as permissible by teachers at the mosque, since obedience to teachers was also required in Islam, and Allah would forgive singing in these circumstances.

Incidents of teacher insensitivity and even punishment for not singing were related to us:

> Once there was this teacher and I was not singing because it was this Christian song ... I told her I didn't want to sing it, and she asked me to sing it ... I said I don't want to sing because I'm not a Christian ... So she put me in detention.
> *(Muslim boy, School 1)*

The possibility of avoiding the requirement to sing was put forward by some children as a strong argument for going to an Islamic school:

> Things I don't like in this school and I don't want to do it that way ... I might not have to do it over there.
> Interviewer: For example?
> Singing ...
> Interviewer: What don't you like about singing?
> I hate it, because Muslims are not allowed to sing.
> *(Muslim boy, School 3)*

Children also recognised that school was the location for numerous incidents and conflicts which they defined as racism. Here we concentrate only on how children describe the way such issues are managed by the school as an institution. Overall they were aware of and supported policies which value all children equally.

> Like Muslims and that ... The school make sure we all get tret [treated] the same ... The school makes sure you never say that it is only white people can come or something.
> *(White Christian girl, School 1)*

But they are also aware that conflicts between children sometimes have, or take on, an ethnic or religious dimension, and express anger if staff fail to recognise this, or unfairly support the people that 'started it', and discipline the victims. For example, in School 2 we heard of lack of action over conflicts between Muslim and Sikh boys:

> Boy 1: And some Muslims even they say bad things about our religion sometimes ... just because there are less of us and more of them ...
> Boy 2: Somehow I can't take it ... I shall just beat em up ... I really can't take it ...
> Interviewer: Hit em back eh?
> Boy 1: Yes ... I'll chase em until they run out of energy and then I'll kick them ...
> Boy 2: The dinner ladies ... if somebody hits you and you tell them they say ... why don't you just go and play nicely ...
> Boy 1: The dinner ladies they don't listen to us.
> Boy 2: They don't do anything.
> Boy 1: They don't do anything even if they are the same religion right ... even if someone is being racist they don't care ... they don't care unless you involve them ... unless you are fighting and stuff.
> *(Two Sikh boys, School 2)*

And in one school two girls felt the (white) head was biased against white children:

> Girl 1: All the girls wanted to play a game ... and all the Muslims wanted to play football and they got to play to football ... and all the Muslims said we can't play football ... this is our own country ... and they said go back to your [country?] and we said go back to India ...
> Girl 2: And then they got X [head teacher] ... and X ... did something ... X never does anything when we complain.
> *(Two white Christian girls)*

Friendships and social circles at school

We locate this discussion in the context of the school because it was there that we collected almost all our data, and it is there that children probably spend the largest part of their time, in the company of other children from a single age cohort of the population of the neighbourhood. All other things being equal, therefore, children in a school with a mixed and unselective intake should find it possible to form relationships with a wide range of children, irrespective of gender, ethnicity and religious affiliation. We need to note that children living in neighbourhoods where a single ethnic or religious group forms a huge majority of the population, or attending a school which tends to select only from one religious background, may not have such opportunities. Of course, even in a mixed school, all other things are unlikely to be equal, as we shall now see.

Given that schools group children into academic years, it is hardly surprising that the majority of relationships mentioned were with those of the same age as themselves. There were, however, examples of friends from different years, which was often due to children knowing each other outside of school and/or being related. When relationships outside school time were listed, older and younger children often featured, including siblings, cousins (often referred to by South Asian background children as cousin-brothers/cousin-sisters) and friends from religion-based or other leisure activities. Friendships tended to be same-sexed with some gender-mixing in groups and a small minority talking about boyfriend/girlfriend relationships.

In all three schools mixing across cultures and religions was evident at least for some children and in some contexts. However, it was also the case that many friendship circles were religio-ethnically homogeneous, particularly in the two schools in Northcity and especially for those Muslim children in whose lives religion plays a central part. These patterns and their social meanings did not go unnoticed by other children. Muslim and non-Muslim children were aware that some Muslim children associated more or less exclusively with other Muslims. Although there were some examples of groupings of children who were entirely white and Christian (in School 1 and in the case of the girls in School 3) these tended not to be referred to in terms of ethnicity, and still less in terms of religion.

Before trying to categorise patterns of relationship, we need to consider what children actually mean when they talk about being friends. Clearly, sometimes for some children friendship is an intense personal and emotionally bonded relationship. Several children talked about valuing friends because 'they back you up' or 'make you feel happy', and how it all depends on personality. For others and at other times a friend may simply be someone who is available when you want to do something that requires more than one person. The term 'friend' can be even weaker than this as, for example, in this comment:

> Interviewer: It looks to me from their names that they are all girls, and they look all Muslim.
> Yes.

> Interviewer: Why is that? Do you have friends who are not Muslims?
> Yes I've friends who are not Muslim but I don't usually play with them.
> *(Muslim girl, School 1)*

In this case friendship may be simply a regular and almost accidental association with someone who is fine to talk with, pleasant enough and certainly not hostile, but is not a chosen playmate. Perhaps this arises because there is a plentiful supply of more favoured others, or perhaps because of recognised social differences. Furthermore, different obligations and choices on the use of time, which are shaped by religious affiliation or culture, may present barriers to regular association and the development of strong bonds of friendship.

Children also talked about those they would avoid when considering friendships which included 'people you can't trust', those 'who are rude and push you' and bullies. A typical response was:

> Interviewer: How do you decide who's going to be your friend?
> Personality really. Say someone like one of those people who bullies loads of people, I don't like them. I used to be one of the main targets, but I am not anymore. But those were the days that I hated. I am not friends with those people, they are the people I don't like.
> *(Christian boy, School 1)*

To illustrate the patterns in one school we present the sociogram or network diagram. Figure 3.1 shows the playground interaction as reported by the 24 children from year 6 who completed the worksheets in class. The broad outlines of this diagram correspond quite well to what was observed in the playground and classroom over the fieldwork period of several weeks. Aliases here are given by the researchers, using names which indicate gender and religious affiliation. The most striking factor illustrated by the diagram is the almost total segregation between the genders. Second, there is the division between a core group of six highly observant Muslim boys and the other boys who are a mixed group in terms of ethnicity and religion. (However, it has to be pointed out that in this class there was not a single Muslim girl, and one can only speculate about the network patterns if the gender and religion balance had been different.)

From the diagram, and interview material from all three schools, three main types of social network categories can be identified: one-way friendships; paired friendships; and the group-type social network.

One-way friendships are when a child identifies having friendships in the school which do not seem to be reciprocated by the other named child or children (for

Figure 3.1: School 3 playground network

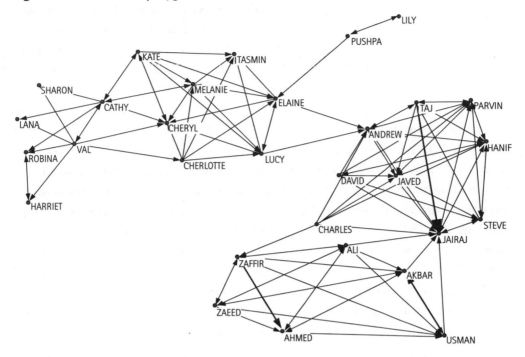

example, Charles in Figure 3.1). Two children across the three schools fell into this category; both are boys who joined their school later than most other children in their classes. These children may or may not be aware of this lack of reciprocation, which may in some cases arise from exclusion from peer groups by other children, on the basis of particular personality issues or unpopularity of the person involved. One of the two boys (a Christian in School 1) illustrated being aware of this: 'I have quite a few friends but most of them don't hardly ever play with me'.

Paired friendships are where two children mutually identified spending most of their time with each other (sometimes extending to time outside school) and may talk about each other as being 'best friends' (for example Pushpa and Lily in Figure 3.1). All the paired friendships we encountered were same sexed. Some of these pairs came from similar religious and ethnic backgrounds, and others were mixed. There were probably more inter-faith pairs in School 2 where diversity was greatest and had given the opportunity for Muslim/Hindu, black Christian/Muslim, Sikh/white Christian and other patterns of relationship to develop over time. Usually paired friendships were acknowledged, and sometimes commented on, by other children. Such pairs were sometimes fairly exclusive of other relationships, but could also occur within the context of larger groups and networks, although in this case they are harder to identify from the outside.

The third category, 'the group', is a social network that includes three or more children who mention spending time together at school. This was the most common type of friendship circle identified by the children in this study (and represented by the three main clusters in Figure 3.1 – described by children themselves as 'the girls', 'the lads' and 'the mosque boys'). Its shape and form is harder to capture than paired friendships, as different children within the same circle of friends had overlapping but not identical friendship circles. Some groups appeared to have quite tight and exclusive boundaries, others to be a cluster within a wider network. Most of the groups only included children from a single year group. The groups were predominantly same sexed, though there was evidence of gender-crossing by a few individuals in some groups, and some teasing interaction between groups of boys and girls. Some groups were religiously mixed, others were not (compare the top right with the bottom right cluster in Figure 3.1). In Schools 1 and 3 the most exclusive groups were composed entirely of Muslim children and the resulting de facto segregation of playground life was recognised by most of the children we talked to, although there were different interpretations. Two Christian girls, for example, talked positively about their relationships with Muslims in the class, and went on to specify friendship with two of the less observant Muslim boys:

> Girl 1: I don't see why we have to be separated from different religions.
> Girl 2: We all mix in our school because most of the boys are like Muslims and ...
> Girl 1: So we just get a long with them ...
> Girl 2: Yeah we just play with them ...
> Girl 1: We don't think of like they're Muslims so we can't play with them, we just play with them.
> *(Two Christian girls, School 3)*

In contrast, two highly observant Muslim boys indicated they felt excluded from association outside their own group:

> Boy 1: We play with Hindus sometimes ...
> Interviewer: But you tend mainly to play with Muslims ...
> Boy 2: Yeah.
> Interviewer: Have you ever had any Christian friends?
> Boy 1: No ...
> Interviewer: Why not?
> Boy 2: We don't get a chance ... they won't play with us Muslims.
> *(Two Muslim boys, School 3)*

However, friendship circles were fluid, with movement occurring within and across the different types of social circles, with children constantly negotiating and renegotiating social interactions depending on the situation and context that they found themselves in. For example, during the absence of a paired friend, one girl spent part of her break times with a family friend in year 5, part on her own, and some time with a group of girls in her class whom she also spent time with at breakfast club. One of the girls that she played with mentioned this:

> Interviewer: And did you play with the same people?
> Girl 1: Yeah.
> Girl 2: But we normally play with X and Y cos Z's friend was away so we were playing with Z today ... she's our friend.
> *(Two Christian girls, School 3)*

Fluidity of association should not be confused with the notion that children's friendships are short-lived and forever changing. Some children talked about having arguments and falling out with friends; however, this was not necessarily the end of their friendship. Furthermore, when children mentioned the history of their friendships, more often than not these were traced back to reception or nursery or even earlier. There was evidence to suggest that some children changed friendships, although this was not reported often and when it was, it was usually in reference to another person: 'there's a girl S, she changes her best friends everyday ... when she first came she liked O. Then Z, then l, then me, then l, then N, then me, and then U, then L, then me, and now L. She keeps on swapping' (Hindu girl, School 2).

Gender, religion and friendship

It is widely believed, and has often been shown by research, that children in the 9 to 11 age group spend much of their time in single-sex peer group activity. We should also note that in a Muslim environment this is also the age group where many activities tend to become separated by gender, and the strength of this was reflected by the fact that, in the network mapping exercise, not a single Muslim child listed a relationship with a schoolmate of the opposite gender. We observed interaction, recorded children's friendship choices, and heard the children's own accounts of social patterns in which same-sex relationships predominated across all types of children. This is not to say that there was no interaction or a total absence of friendships between boys and girls in the school context. However, the public discourse of children about the opposite sex tended to set boys and girls up in opposition to each other. For example, teasing or derogatory comments were made, by both boys and girls:

> Interviewer: Are there any kids in the class who you don't play with or don't get on with?
> Boy 1: The girls.
> Interviewer: The girls, what's wrong with the girls?
> Boy 1: They are ugly.
> Boy 2: Sometimes they spoil things ... we wind them up.
> *(Two Christian boys, School 3)*

> Interviewer: What's wrong with the boys?
> Christian girl: They bug me ... they are typical ...
> Interviewer: What's typical about boys? ... I was a boy once ...
> Christian girl: They are boys ...
> Interviewer: What's wrong with them?
> Christian girl: They are boys ...
> Interviewer: There must be a reason?
> Christian girl: They are boys ...
> Hindu girl: They are boys ...
> Interviewer: What do boys do that bugs you?
> Hindu girl: They always want to spoil our games and make jokes.
> *(Christian girl and Hindu girl, School 3)*

On the other hand, some of the Christian girls (unprompted) expressed strong interest in boys as potential, and actual, 'boyfriends'. Although they said race or religion would not be a barrier for them, they implicitly or explicitly seemed to rule out Muslim boys who were extensively involved in religion. In School 3 they spoke about a particular Muslim boy who was less observant and classed as one of 'the lads', and admitted that at least one girl 'fancied' or had even 'gone out with' him. They commented that such relationships are difficult because 'his mother doesn't want him to go out with a white girl'. Boys, however, were less likely to talk about girls in this way and some Muslim boys tended to become particularly embarrassed if asked anything about girls in the class.

Racism, religion and conflict

Several children (across all ethnic groups including whites) told us they found it hard to get on with others who they considered to be racist, or behaving in a racist way. We heard about (and witnessed) some fights both within school and in the street. These for the most part did not involve children of different religious or ethnic backgrounds. However, some children did tell us of such 'racialised' conflict in school and, more often, out in the community.

> Interviewer: Is there aggro between Muslim kids and white kids?
> Girl 1: Yes there is, because all the Muslims they hang around together and they say stuff about white kids ... which I can't say to you because you will tell the teacher ...
> Interviewer: I said I won't tell ...
> Girl 1: They said that F***ing white ...
> Girl 2: Donkey ...
> *(Two Christian girls, School 3)*

> Boy 1: We've had fights with other children ... calling people names and everything?
> Interviewer: People call you names sometimes?
> Boy 1: People do ... they call me like they do ... they say racist things ...
> Boy 2: They go 'paki' and everything.
> Boy 1: They say to me 'Bin Laden'.
> *(Two Muslim boys, School 1)*

However, two friends (a Hindu girl and an observant Christian girl) commented about children sometimes saying things they don't really mean:

> Interviewer: Would you say that it is not racist in your school because it is mixed?
> Hindu girl: No. Like there's some ... not much ... people that fight and they just say it.
> Christian girl: They say it, they don't mean it but they just say it to try and hurt someone.
> Interviewer: Can you give me an example?
> Hindu girl: One person fighting a different race say an Asian and a Christian and then when they're fighting one of them calls him ??? then it becomes a big argument ...
> Christian girl: And then one blames it on someone else and say oh you called me this first.
> *(Hindu girl and Christian girl, School 3)*

This type of comment, combined with other comments in the data, tends to support the view that children generally think of relationships as being built out of a series of personal interactions, and choices made by individual social actors. While they do recognise that wider social structures and norms (for example those linked with race, gender and religion) can impinge on social situations, for the most part they do not see these as determining the nature of their own individual relationships. Many of the children were aware of and used the terms 'racist' and 'racism' as powerful language to critique behaviour that they found unacceptable and which they interpreted as being based on ethnic or religious difference. Clearly the perception of racism, or the labelling of incidents as racist, can have consequences as significant as the incident itself. The contrast between the ethnic term 'Asian' and the religious term 'Christian', both used here as markers of racial difference, underline how the categories of ethnicity and religion overlap and have fuzzy boundaries in the children's discourse. However, terms such as religious discrimination or Islamophobia were not used by any of the children.

On the basis of the evidence in this section our key findings are that:

- Children appreciated that primary schools (regardless of their religious status) played a role in bringing children of different religions together. Many of them valued the opportunity to mix across cultures and learn about these differences.
- However, despite official commitment to valuing diversity, some school policies and practices reinforced informal segregation and, in some children's views, failed to deal adequately with conflicts between groups marked by religious/ethnic difference. There were some issues where some children felt that they, the group they identified with, and/or their religion were not being treated fairly.
- School is a setting which allows friendships between children of different backgrounds to develop. However, identity issues in which religion may play a part within locally specific ethnic group dynamics mean there may be divisions, conflicts and patterns of exclusion which children recognise.

4. Research findings 3: believing and belonging beyond school

In this section we consider the children's accounts of their lifestyles beyond the school gate. We look specifically at the role played by religion in shaping these lifestyles, and consider whether religious difference may play a part in segregating children's lives.

Time outside school structured by religion

Children's accounts show lives overlap at school, and friendships across religions and ethnic groups do develop there for some. However, schoolfriends and classmates may or may not share time and space outside the school context. How children spend their time out of school is to varying degrees organised by their family circumstances, and by their religious commitments and practices. They may have different patterns in terms of the use of time, of space in the home and neighbourhood, and in terms of consumption of material goods, services and entertainment. Where these patterns diverge, the children who follow them may find they have little opportunity to spend time with each other out of school, even if they wish to do so. Finally, in the setting of a wider culture where there are significant levels of racism and intolerance and growing evidence of religious difference becoming a marker for hostility between groups, most clearly in the phenomenon of Islamophobia, it is not inconceivable that children may be actively discouraged by adults from mixing across the religions.

Assuming children spend about 35 hours in school each week and have about 70 hours for sleep and so on, 60 hours per week (and more during school holidays) are available for other purposes. However, it is not possible to designate this all as 'spare time' since for some children routines like commuting, visiting absent parents, helping with domestic chores and homework reduce the time available. The biggest lifestyle difference linked to religion between children in our sample was that between the very observant Muslim children and the rest. The former typically spent

15 to 20 hours per week involved in religious instruction, and an additional hour or more each day involved in the rituals around the daily prayer times, and in doing homework for the classes at mosque.

This description of the time spent at mosque was slightly atypical as it included weekend as well as weekday evening sessions:

> Interviewer: Do you go there [the mosque] every day?
>
> Boy 1: Every evening ... [from 5pm to 7.30pm]
>
> Boy 2: And Saturdays and Sundays as well ...
>
> Interviewer: Weekends as well ...
>
> Boy 1: I go for about an hour I have to pray ... I have to read in the mosque.
>
> *(Two Muslim boys, School 1)*

For those that did not attend a mosque for classes, private tuition amounting to only a few hours per week was often carried out at home. Given the amount of time spent in mosque it was unsurprising to find an absence of highly observant Muslim children reporting playing out, or attending secular after-school activities, or regularly viewing children's TV programmes. When they did play out it was usually with other Muslim children on the way to or on the way back from mosque:

> Interviewer: Do you play out in the streets as well?
>
> Boy 1: Hardly, we don't have hardly any time ...
>
> Interviewer: Maybe in the summer you have a bit more time to do that?
>
> Boy 2: Yes because when we come back from mosque it's still light ...
>
> Boy 1: Or if we come a bit early from mosque ...
>
> Interviewer: So who do you play with when you are out in the streets?
>
> Boy 2: I play with him.
>
> Interviewer: Any others?
>
> Boy 1: I play with him in summer and with H [another Muslim boy] ... we play football ... or cricket.
>
> *(Two Muslim boys, School 1)*

The amount of time spent attending mosque meant that it was unlikely that highly observant Muslim and less observant children would share the same play or leisure time and space outside of the school context. As one Muslim boy described, the only time he got to see his white friends was when they crossed paths between leaving and going to different after-school activities.

The pattern of daily ritual for Muslims that many of the children described involves a fivefold observance of prayer (namaz), which can take place in any suitable room or open space. Many men and boys choose to use a local mosque, while females usually perform this at home. Before each prayer time each believer goes through a process of ritual washing (wudhu), and this is also required when touching or reading the Holy Quran. There is also a preference to change into suitable Islamic clothes before performing prayers. Boys wear hats and a long shirt over trousers that are cut to cover below the knee but to show the ankle. A girl described her clothing thus:

> Interviewer: What are your mosque clothes?
> Girl: You have to wear all white.
> Interviewer: All white what?
> Girl: Um like its like a dress on top. A long dress and scarf.
> *(Muslim girl, School 2)*

Two boys described their evening routine in detail:

> Boy 1: I just go home ... and go upstairs and get changed into my mosque clothes, and I have to do this thing called 'wuzu' yeah ...
> Interviewer: What does that mean?
> Boy 2: You have to wash your face and hands ...
> Boy 1: You have to wash your hands three times ... then you have to gargle your mouth three times ... then get your little finger and do that, put water up your nose, then get your little finger and do that, clean your mouth ... then you wash your face three times, then you get your middle finger and your other finger and you go over your head like that and you go behind your ears then you wipe it on your neck ... and if you have washed your arms three times both of them and your legs, and both feet three times ... you put this clothes thing on ... called 'chuppa' and you put a hat on ... a mosque hat on ... and you have this thing called Holy Quran and you take that with you to mosque, and you go and pray for two hours, then I come back and I go to my room or I play out for half an hour.
> *(Two Muslim boys, School 3)*

The Muslim children we spoke to were all familiar with these routines, both for adults in their families and for themselves, and many performed them daily, although because the timing of prayers, several of them said they only did their namaz three times daily.

> Interviewer: How often does [your dad] go to mosque?
> Girl 1: He goes Monday to Friday, um five times. I don't think he really reads fajr all the time. But when he's out all day, when he's at work he can't go to the mosque.

> Girl 2: My grandmother's more, because she's always like waking up for fajr, and she always prays and keeps on reading the Quran. My dad yeah, he always goes mosque to read on Fridays, jumma namaz, but mostly he reads at home. And my mum she does read but sometimes she misses zuhr and fajr cos she's got loads of work to do for the house.
> Interviewer: What about you and your brothers and sisters?
> Girl 2: I don't read fajr.
> Girl 1: I can't read fajr or zuhr because I'm at school. But only sometimes like, um Fridays I always read. But the rest of the days I don't [except] when there's like a programme in the mosque ...
> *(Two Muslim girls, School 2)*

The pattern of time structured through religious instruction classes, daily prayer rituals and seasonal rituals such as the Ramadan fast were experiences that were recognised as being shared with other Muslim children, not only in the locality but in other British cities, and probably across the Islamic world.

In contrast even the most observant of the Christian, Sikh and Hindu children experienced a much less intense and less time-consuming pattern of devotion – typically no more than weekly attendance at a class for religious or language instruction, and/or public act of worship, plus a brief time of prayer or worship at a domestic shrine or round a family meal table. Hindu children might also be involved in, or be aware of older family members who followed a pattern of weekly ritual observance involving partial fasting, or abstinence from certain foods or activities such as haircuts on specific days.

> Interviewer: What sort of religious things do you do at home?
> Boy: There is a mini temple in our house ... and we even pray there ... if we don't have time to go ...
> Interviewer: So who leads the prayers there? How do you do it? Do you do it individually?
> Boy: Individually any time we want ... My dad does it is on the days that I told you when I don't eat meat ... Monday.
> Interviewer: Which are those days you don't eat meat?
> Boy: I don't eat ... I eat it sometimes. ... But Monday Thursday and Saturday ... And we have a day when we have to eat cold food ... the food has to be cold.
> *(Hindu boy, School 3)*

Religious buildings

Children often talked to us about local places of worship as familiar landmarks, and places where they, or their friends, took part in activities. There were children who rarely or never visited, or attended, a place of worship, and others for whom a local place of worship was an important venue in their lives and where they spent many hours each week. In both Northcity and Eastborough there were many local places of worship for all the major religions. Although many children attended these, in School 2 there were also several whose families 'belonged' to a church or temple some distance away or even on the other side of London.

Religious buildings sometimes had a sacred and almost supernatural significance for children. A group discussion talked about the huge parish church across the road from School 3. The church itself had long been disused, while the congregation meets for worship in the school hall or presbytery. At the time it was in the early stages of a redevelopment project to convert it into a leisure/training/childcare centre for the whole local community. Many of the children felt the redevelopment of the old church was an inappropriate use for a religious building and would have preferred it to be restored for use as a church because, as a Hindu boy put it, 'a holy man (the parish priest) lives there'. With a contrasting sense of the numinous, one pair of Muslim girls described part of the mosque where funeral rites often took place as a scary and spooky place, haunted by devils.

Although references to visits mostly concerned places of worship where people 'belonged', several children talked of episodes where they had visited places of worship from a religion other than their own. Taking part in sports, educational and leisure activities at community centres managed by a religious organisation was the most frequent event whereby children and their families of all religious backgrounds had entered Christian, Hindu or Sikh 'territory'. In addition, some children had accompanied a friend to an act of worship, such as a Muslim girl in School 1 who had gone to church with a Christian friend and stood at the back. Another Hindu child in School 2 spoke of a Christian auntie who often took them to her church. Others had visited places of worship for a special community event, or as a tourist, such as the Muslim boy whose father had taken him to look round a Christian church and a Jewish synagogue in Karachi. One Sikh girl told us she and her family sometimes offered worship in a Hindu temple. However, it appeared quite rare for non-Muslim children to pay visits to or use facilities in mosques. This seems to underline the reality of a degree of segregation between communities in the neighbourhood and a sense of the 'other people's territory' around some places of worship. Indeed, in Northcity we heard of a few incidents where Christian children had entered a mosque in unanticipated circumstances, one in pursuit of a lost ball, another, a girl from School 3, egged on to creep in by her brother only to find that 'a man was chasing me with a stick [yelling] "comeback, comeback now girl"', and a third, also a girl from School 3, only because: 'an adult Muslim came and kicked my friend ... and her mum came out and she was really mad, so she went into the mosque and complained ... and they got justice ... and she got some money ...'.

Only a very few children spoke of going to local places of worship on a school visit, which suggests the schools may not be making much use of them as local resource for the RE curriculum.

Attending worship

The majority of white (nominally Christian) children interviewed did not attend Sunday worship on a regular basis. A small number of the white children and all the black Christian children we spoke to, were regular attenders at some church. A few children, including one Hindu boy, often turned up to Sunday church worship on their own or with friends rather than adults in their family. One of the significant things about the churchgoing children is that denominational differences had hardly any significance. With the exception of one Mormon and one strict Evangelical child, they found it hard to name (correctly) the denomination of the church they attended, or to describe the differences between Christian churches, except sometimes by reference to the architecture of the building, or the practices and rituals of worship. Children's experience in church typically consisted of groups or classes specifically designed for children, which they mostly enjoyed. However, in Roman Catholic churches children were likely to attend adult oriented parish mass, in which many of the girls we talked to played a significant role as 'servers' dressed in special robes:

> Girl 1: We are altar servers.
> Interviewer: What does that mean?
> Girl 2: And we help Father M...
> Girl 1: We help Father M... out ... Plus we do christenings and that.
> Interviewer: So what does that mean, does it mean going to church on Sunday?
> Girl 1: Yes.
> Girl 2: I used to go on Saturday but I have stopped doing it now, because I ain't got time ...

> Girl 1: She has to do it by herself and it's really hard for her ... the I am in a group ... because we used to be in a group ...
> Girl 2: I can still be in to the group Father M... said
> Girl 1: I do do it ... Sometimes I go just to watch the mass but sometimes Father M... needs me to serve, so every time I go I in end up serving every time.
> *(Two Catholic girls, School 3)*

On the whole the Muslim children had a much stronger relationship with a local mosque which many attended daily for religious instruction and prayers. Boys might also use the mosque several more times for their prayer times. Girls described a different relationship with the mosque; they too spent many hours in Quran classes, but there were often restrictions on where they could go in the building.

> Girl 1: On Fridays the boys go to pray with ... most everyday sometimes the boys go to pray with the men ... In the side rooms ...
> Girl 2: The girls are not allowed to go in the men's part ... Like when they are praying the ... [unless] if you go in the mosque and the teacher tells us to go ... And like get some water or something then we are allowed to go.
> *(Two Muslim girls, School 3)*

In School 3 the Muslim boys also saw the mosque as a leisure facility, as it had a large car park where they could meet their friends and play football, and offered some youth club rooms where youngsters could play table tennis and pool.

The Hindu and Sikh children we talked to all seemed familiar with religious activities at temples and Gurudwaras but for the most part did not follow as regular a pattern of attendance as the Muslims or churchgoing Christians. We heard accounts of religious rituals, lectures from priests and gatherings at festivals and weddings which often included communal meals. The children said they had a fair degree of freedom to drop in and out of the temple ceremonies as they pleased, they could sit quietly with the adults or go out and chat or 'mess about' with their friends, as long as their behaviour was reasonably good and respectful: 'I just go and sit inside the temple ... just you have to sit there and [listen?] but I don't really do that, my mum does that. I go upstairs and talk to my friends and I play inside ... I go to my classroom, go and mess about' (Hindu girl, School 3).

The temples and Gurudwaras were also important to the children for leisure and sports activities. Some of the boys were involved in football teams which had occasional trips for matches against temples in other parts of the country: 'There is a youth club there and I've joined ... There is like a football team, and we are going to go to London and play a five-a-side match ... it's against another temple ... it's on 26th July ... and I've been picked to play' (Hindu boy, School 3).

Some of the girls were involved in dancing groups at a temple, although they might not like the style in comparison with 'normal' dance:

> I went like once ... dancing at the temple but I didn't really like it because it was a bit too different ... I'm not into classical dancing and things like, just normal ... and I've done a bit of Indian Classical Dancing but I don't really enjoy doing it cos it's really hard and you've got to try and make animals with your hands.
> *(Hindu girl, School 3)*

Clubs run by religious organisations

Many children among those who did not have daily sessions at mosque went to one or more regular organised leisure activities or clubs in the evenings or at weekends. For some attendance was time limited or episodic; as one child said 'I went a few times but then it got boring'. Within this range of activity groups, school-based clubs, after-school childcare agencies and secular sporting activities were important. However, many youth clubs, uniformed organisations (cubs, brownies etc.), dance and drama classes and sports activities were associated with religion if only because they were held in halls linked with churches, temples or Gurudwaras. The only activities which had a clear religious content were church choirs or music groups, or midweek fun clubs run by evangelical churches. These were especially significant for many of the white children in Northcity, including several who did not attend Sunday worship at the church that ran the club.

> Interviewer: So let's talk about this cool kids' club on Friday evening ... what sort of things happen?
> Boy: They do songs about God and stuff ... and worshipping God ... And you do games and you can mess around ... You can have a good time ... and then it finishes at half past eight ... And it starts at five, and after cool kids' club if you are in secondary school you can go to youth club ...
> *(Catholic boy, School 3)*

Religious instruction classes

The churchgoing children from Protestant or evangelical communities generally received very low-key religious instruction in the context of children's groups running alongside Sunday worship for adults. Mostly they regarded these activities as a fun club for children, with some Bible stories, drawing and singing thrown in. The most demanding academic activity we heard of was the task of memorising a short Bible verse:

> There was a children's part for like playing ... you could go in there but you didn't have to ... that's why ... like there's a children's part and like a proper church you could either stay in there and pray ... But you know the children who don't know how to pray and all that could go and play in the other ... I enjoyed it because it was fun and you have to like draw pictures of God and we read stories and then we acted them.
> *(Christian girl, School 1)*

The Roman Catholic pattern was commonly that of short-term religious instruction (as a Saturday class) for a period of a month or two prior to initiation, via first communion. Again the children's accounts suggested the learning involved was not very demanding, and the children told us how the commitment was made worthwhile by promised rewards, such as an outing or a weekly youth club night for those who completed the course. One or two reported their dislike of the discipline imposed in one class when a nun shouted at them in order to stop noisy chattering. 'Every Saturday [for a month] you went to the parish house ... and you did activities about stuff ... You have to learn about Moses and you have to eat unleavened bread ... And one about three weeks ago they took us to farm animal world and it's near L... and the beach' (Catholic boy, School 3).

Hindu children often reported that they regularly attended heritage language classes (usually in Gujerati), at the weekend at a local temple or Hindu centre. The language teaching was quite serious and hard work, with a graded examination system through which they progressed. Children attending these lessons did not seem very enthusiastic and tended to describe them as boring and too strict. Religion and ethics were only a small and largely incidental part of the learning, for example a story or reading book might be based on a Hindu legend or myth, or a song might be a devotional one. One boy told us that the religious content of his lessons amounted to 'be nice and don't hit people'. Sikh children in some cases attended or had attended Punjabi language classes at the local Gurudwara, where some of the content might have religious reference. More significant, perhaps, was the fact that children who were knowledgeable about the Sikh religion said they had learned many stories at home, usually as told or read to them by their mother.

For many Muslim children there were classes for three hours at least five times each week at a local mosque, or sometimes in a 'house that prays'. Almost all of them accepted that this pattern of intensive and serious religious and moral instruction within a strict learning environment was a natural part of their Islamic identity, and many of them accepted and owned what they had been taught as true and worthy of obedience. Several also said it was good fun to be with their friends at these classes.

> Interviewer: Do you like going to mosque?
> Boy: Yeah.
> Interviewer: Yeah, tell me why.
> Boy: Because you see all your friends. Talk to them.
> *(Muslim boy, School 2)*

However, many of them found the sheer time commitment a burden, and looked with envy at 'Christians [who] have it easy' and have far more time for fun and play, especially in the school holidays:

> Boy: Most of the time out of school I'm feeling quite ill, really tired ...
> Interviewer: Why, are you working too hard at school?
> Boy: ... mosque ... I've got to go to mosque at ... and my ears start hurting 'n everything because people are praying too loud.
> *(Muslim boy, School 1)*

The lessons they spoke of were based on learning to read the Holy Quran in its original Arabic, leading up to the possibility of learning to recite the whole text by heart (becoming hafiz), and only secondarily of trying to understand (and apply) the meaning of the scripture by means of 'kitabs' which offered some translation and explanation in Urdu, Gujerati or English. Instruction, as described to us, was usually based on traditional methods of whole class repetition of the texts after the teacher, with daily testing of the previous lessons. According to a doctoral student working in this area, within the Islamic tradition, these are not merely teaching methods which have become traditional – they are bound up with what Muslims see as the nature of truth, particularly that found in the Quran, which is more than a text. It is a sonoral experience. Such methods are, of course, familiar to a generation of people educated in England as late as the 1960s (for example, spelling tests, times tables, conjugations of Latin verbs, learning and reciting poems) and are perhaps finding a degree of renewed favour among parents and some educationalists today.

Boy 1: When we are memorising the Quran off by heart ... we have to ... go
Saturday but the other classes who are not memorising it they don't go.
Interviewer: So you are trying to become hafiz?
Boy 2: Yes.
Interviewer: ... tell me about your mosque class. How many people are
there there?
Boy 2: There's 13 or 14 people in my class. We have to do three things a
day in mosque ... One is the lesson they gave us the day before ... if we can
learn that off by heart and pray ... then that's the lesson and then after that
lesson we have to do the last seven lessons we have learned off by heart ...
and then after that we have to learn the 14 lessons off by heart and pray ...
Interviewer: You have to do that every day?
Boy 2: Yes.
Interviewer: And what are these lessons about then?
Boy 1: They are just lessons from the Quran ... we have to learn them off by
heart ...
Interviewer: Explain to me a little bit more what it's about?
Boy 1: It's in Arabic.
Interviewer: Do you understand it?
Boy 1: I don't I don't ... it's like if you go on [another] course it's a
different thing ... first you become hafiz ... if you want to know what the
Quran means like in translating into another language ... Then you have to
go on another course and you can learn it off and learn the meaning of the
Quran. Hafiz is just learning it in Arabic ...
Interviewer: Do the teachers try to explain it to you?
Boy 2: They just give it to you ...
(Two Muslim boys, School 2)

Many children spoke of serious amounts of homework needed to memorise their
lessons. Children described the environment they learned in as very different from
their primary school, with carpets, no desks and shoes left outside. Most of the
Muslim children had begun their attendance at mosque classes at or even before the
age of five, and had steadily moved up through the classes, often taking great pride
in their progression. As they got older it was more likely that boys and girls were
taught in separate classes. They told us most of the mosques had a system of tests or
examinations, and in some cases ceremonies and public presentations to reward
achievement. Some children took great pride in their success in these exams.

... we go to the mosque ... and eat and stuff ... We go and children do the
ceremony call ... Jelsa ... And children take part in it ... And I took part

> about bonfire night ... and it is a speech you learn by heart ... Two or three
> pages of writing it ... you learn by heart and then you say it ... you get
> money for doing it ... and then the lesson ... That is when you get the
> present ... and the exam and they tell you the results ... The person who
> comes first gets the best prize ... and the second and third get the same
> prize ...
> *(Muslim girl, School 1)*

Other Muslim children told us there were some mosque teachers who were liked and
admired, and at least one child aspired to become one when grown up. However,
children frequently talked about the strict discipline they encountered at mosque,
and some explicitly expressed concerns and ambivalence about practices which they
compared unfavourably with their experience in day school. Several told us they
hated it when teachers got angry and shouted at them, or they were punished for
talking to classmates or for failure to learn. Many discussed with us the fact that
punishment in some, but by no means all, mosques involved children being hit with
a stick on the back or hands, or being made to stand or squat in uncomfortable
positions for long periods.

> Interviewer: And is the teacher nice or horrible?
> Boy: He's nice.
> Interviewer: Okay, what's nice about him?
> Boy: He doesn't hit you.
> Interviewer: That's good. Do most of the mosques hit?
> Boy: Not all the mosques, some of them. Strict ones.
> *(Muslim boy, School 2)*

A few children told us that they laughed about it, or that it didn't hurt as they had
got used to it, and one girl told us about the time she had literally 'taken the rap' for
a friend. In contrast, two boys when discussing this actually asked if hitting was
allowed:

> Boy 1: We read the Holy Book ... the Quran ... and then we go to the Mauli
> Sahib and if we make mistakes he hits ...
> Interviewer: He hits you?
> Boy 1: Yes.
> Boy 2: With sticks.
> Boy 1: Yes.
> Interviewer: And that happens at your mosque as well?
> Boy 2: Yes.
> Boy 1: Is that allowed?

Interviewer: Pardon?

Boy 2: Is that allowed to hit? ...

Interviewer: What do you think about that?

Boy 2: They shouldn't because if you get like lots of mistakes the more he beats you ... and if you do it early on and do it they won't hit you ... but if you are last he will do that ... so it's better that you keep reading and don't let ...

Interviewer: It sounds very different from school.

Boy 2: Yes.

Interviewer: How would you say it's different?

Boy 1: In school they don't boss you and in mosque they do ...

(Two Muslim boys, School 2)

We were told several times that children felt nothing could be done about it because parents fully supported the regime, and it was suggested that things might be worse in some Islamic boarding schools where parents could not see what was going on.

Interviewer: What do your parents think about it?

Boy 1: The parents don't care ... like it's our fault if we don't know it ...

Boy 2: They tell the teachers to hit us ...

(Two Muslim boys, School 3)

Having described the children's accounts of their experience it is important to make several points about the wider context, in order to put the issue of discipline and corporal punishment into perspective. Only a generation ago the majority of mainstream schools in the UK regularly resorted to caning or other forms of corporal punishment to maintain discipline, and it is only a decade or so since such punishment was banned. Even now the majority of British parents believe in and practise smacking small children and public opinion is probably against legislation curtailing parents' freedom to chastise their offspring. Some Christians and independent Christian schools continue to argue for what they would see as the right and duty of parents not to 'spare the rod' on the basis of their religious beliefs and reading of scripture. And as we have seen, some Hindu and Christian children find that discipline in classes outside mainstream school is uncomfortably stricter than inside. The evidence from Muslim children in our research, and wider knowledge of Muslim communities across the UK, suggests that many mosques and madressas are catching up with legislation which outlaws corporal punishment in schools. It is also said that some parents are voting with their feet by arranging private religious tutors at home rather than subject their children to strict discipline in the local mosque. A new generation of British-born religious teachers is emerging who are more familiar with alternatives than were the imams who often came from rural Pakistan or Bangladesh and spoke little English. Many Muslim leaders, umbrella organisations such as the Lancashire Council of Mosques and those working in partnership with the London Borough of Redbridge (2003) are taking a lead in promoting the introduction of child protection policies in their member bodies. For most of the children who talked to us about these matters, change cannot come too soon.

Entries and exits

Initiation rites were mentioned, mostly by Christian children who had been involved personally or as a spectator in christenings, baptisms or first communion celebrations. One evangelical Christian girl spoke about being 'saved' and subsequently being baptised by total immersion along with her sister, and another from a Mormon family described baptism and other initiation rites in her own church. A Sikh boy described a naming ritual as 'like a baptism'.

For many of the Roman Catholic children first communion was especially significant or salient in their minds as it was a recent or imminent event in their lives. It involved dressing up in special smart clothes, 'like I was getting married', and for some at least it has a religious significance marking 'kind of being in more into Christ, Christian reality'. In some cases, especially in Eastborough, it was tied up with the processes of choosing a 'good' secondary school, and had not been completed soon enough to gain a place at one of the popular local Catholic highschools.

Conversations about death and funeral rites were limited, suggesting that most of the children had had few encounters with death. In fact conversations about funerals of rabbits and hamsters were more numerous in the data than those of humans, although confined to white Christian or no religion children. Several Muslim boys spoke of visits to the cemetery at Eid. A couple of children with a Roman Catholic background spoke of family celebrations or rituals on the anniversary of the death of a departed relative.

Several children found ghosts, 'scary stuff' and the supernatural to be of great fascination. Two Muslim girls gave several extensive accounts of vernacular stories, beliefs and practices involving ghosts, demons, supernatural events and exorcism rituals conducted by holy men (*pirs*). These accounts were clearly based on stories they had heard and situations they had been involved with, both in Britain and India, and suggests they were aware of a cultural tradition and spirit world that is rarely discussed in accounts of mainstream Islam.

Religious festivals

Children from all the different religions have a common experience of festivals as mainly about presents, money, food, fun and parties, breaks from school and family gatherings. Only a minority (mostly Muslims) seemed able to talk about the religious significance of festivals or the stories behind them. In School 3, for example, only one child in a classroom session seemed to be aware of the seasonal significance of hot cross buns as a reminder of Christ's crucifixion. As one Hindu boy saw it, festivals were about 'our God's birthday ... and stuff'.

There were a number of references to taking part in cross-faith celebration of festivals. Some of this is undoubtedly a result of the RE curriculum and celebrations in school, although some of the children were clearly referring to celebrations at home or at a place of worship. Christmas and Easter were marked by children from all religions and none, at least by the giving of presents and Easter eggs, although there were some Muslim children who said firmly that they were not allowed to celebrate Christmas and that its only significance was as a time for bargain hunting in the shops. A pagan boy received presents but gave Christmas an alternative spiritual significance. Some Hindus spoke of the priest in temple publicly retelling the Christian nativity story and of their community gathering to mark Christmas Day. Sikhs, Christians and one Muslim girl also gave accounts of joining in Hindu celebrations at Diwali, in such activities as dancing, mehndi hand painting, fireworks parties, sharing food and sweets.

Unstructured activity at home

All the children we talked to, and those who completed out of school diaries, did spend a considerable amount of time at home, although this varied along with individual and religion structured lifestyles. Most of them gave us the impression that they had ample amounts of adult-free time when they could chose to play or 'chill out' as they pleased. A very high proportion of them had access to some form of electronic games equipment, and time spent playing on these machines was popular across the religions and genders. Indeed, the PS2 or Xbox was sometimes listed as a significant member of the household in network diagrams. TV and video watching was also common (children's programmes, soaps, MTV, 'Indian stuff') although some Muslims do not watch much, or even any, TV, partly because they have little time left after mosque, but in some cases because TV is considered a corrupting un-Islamic influence. According to one child, TV is haram, while another (who did have TV at home) said 'they call it the devil's box'. Another conversation indicates that some homes operate a compromise rather than an absolute ban.

> Girl 1: ... really we are not allowed to watch TV ... but I have got TV.
>
> Girl 2: Really you are not allowed to watch TV at namaz times ...
>
> Girl 1: And we are not allowed to have TV anyway ... cos the prophet he never used to have TV ... so we believe we are not to have TV ...
>
> Girl 2: like when someone has died you are not allowed to watch TV ... no way you can't ...
>
> Girl 1: Cos then we would get like bad sin and that ... so we have to get a cloth and cover the TV and cover all the stuff with eyes and everything ... and that time was so sad because my uncle, my granddad died.
>
> *(Two Muslim girls, School 3)*

Similarly music (usually pop) and dance were important to some, especially white and black girls, and a few children were learning instruments or sang in a church choir. Many of the Muslim children told us music was not allowed in Islam. Pets (hamsters, rabbits, fish and some cats and dogs) are significant for many children but apart from one parrot were not mentioned by Muslim children (dogs are considered haram to Muslims, but are sometimes kept by Hindus).

Visiting each others' homes and sleepovers, where one or more friends spent part of a weekend at someone's home, seemed especially significant among the non-Muslim girls in Northcity. Some boys also mentioned sleepovers and some of the Hindu children were also included. In the few cases where Muslim children mentioned visiting or staying at someone else's home it was almost always with kin.

> Interviewer: So what did you do for your birthday – can you remember?
>
> Girl 1: ... I had a sleepover after and we watched some films and stuff.
>
> Interviewer: So who stayed over at your sleepover?
>
> Girl 1: C, K and my cousin.
>
> Girl 2: Your sister.
>
> Girl 1: And my sister.
>
> Girl 2: And K had her sleepover in April but [Girl 1] couldn't go then could you she was going out.
>
> Interviewer: Do you have sleepovers a lot?
>
> Girl 1: Sometimes we do.
>
> Girl 2: Sometimes but not often.
>
> Girl 1: We're having one soon – we're going to have one in the summer holidays aren't we?
>
> Girl 2: Yeah ...

Interviewer: What do you do during sleepovers?

Girl 1: Well when I went to K's sleepover, her dad was drunk so he burnt all the popcorn but we – well we watched scary films and we tell secrets and things.

Girl 2: And listen to music.

(Two Christian girls, School 3)

Even where are there is a friendship across the religions and an open welcome in each others' home, it is likely that Muslim children will have insufficient time because of attending mosque school. They may also lack confidence that any non-Muslim host family will be able to fulfil the requirements for regular prayer times and halal food. Thus, in the following paired interview one Muslim girl talked about her (white Christian) friend's mother sometimes getting halal food for her when she visited, while the other had not visited such a home.

Girl 1: I've been to J's and S's and I have been to A's house ...

Interviewer: Do you ever eat with them there?

Girl 1: Yes, but because whenever I go they have stuff like ham, I say I don't ... Or I bring money and I go to the shop and get stuff.

Interviewer: So you get something which is halal?

Girl 1: Yes Sometimes J's mum gets halal meat in for me and cooks that and I eat it ...

Interviewer: What about you? Do you have visits and friends from other religions?

Girl 2: I have friends from other religions ... But I'm not really sure that they come to my house ...

Interviewer: Have you been to their houses?

Girl 2: Not really ...

(Two Muslim girls, School 1)

Everyday eating and special food

A final aspect of everyday domestic and social life, which highlighted different experiences and perspectives along religious lines, was food. Diet was recognised by children as having religious significance, and implicitly as having social consequences. Across the religions children often seemed to specify 'junk' foods such as chips, pizza, burgers and sweets as their favourites, and often said they disliked healthy options, such as green vegetables. However, avoidance of particular foods was highly determined by religious factors, and there was at least a vague recognition of these issues by children who saw themselves as being 'allowed to eat anything', which grew as the research progressed in each school.

Many Muslim children talked about halal food, and food that 'we are not allowed to eat' being haram, often specifying items in great detail down to particular E numbers, although they were not always aware where such forbidden foods came from or how they were produced. Two boys describe what they cannot eat:

> Interviewer: And what about the foods that you can't eat ...
> Boy 1: Like pork, ham, some crisps, we can't eat ... gelatine ...
> Interviewer: What's gelatine?
> Boy 1: Sweets ...
> Boy 2: Like if it's got jelly in we can't eat it ... And in the crisps it's like got animal rennet, you can't eat that, whey powder ... there is two sorts of whey powder, there is a vegetarian one and there is a different one ... and E471 ... There are two sorts there is one vegetarian and one not ...
> Boy 1: And also we eat most of the vegetarian crisps ...
> *(Two Muslim boys, School 1)*

These boys continued listing the foods they could not eat including varieties of crisps and particular colours of Smarties. Like almost all Muslim children in this study, they talked very distinctly about foods showing clear and distinct boundaries. They also talked about the restaurants and take-aways where they could eat because they knew the food was halal:

> Interviewer: So what did you put down as your favourite eating place then?
> Boy 1: Dixie fried chicken ... Nice.
> Interviewer: Why is it nice? Is it different from say KFC?
> Boy 1: It's different because at KFC we can't eat most of the things ... because the oil ... they put wine in it ...
> Boy 2: They put beef oil ... and we can't have beef oil ...
> Boy 1: Dixie fried chicken but that's halal.
> Interviewer: How do you know they are halal?
> Boy 1: My [relative] ... he works there ...
> Boy 2: So he made sure it's 100 percent halal ... it's [on a sign?] outside of the shop.
> *(Two Muslim boys, School 1)*

Hindu children were aware of dietary and hygiene rules (not sharing plates), including Hindu traditions of vegetarianism, which some of them followed, at least in part or on special fast days. When prompted some of them talked about not eating beef. Regardless of this, Hindus talked about eating in places that cooked and served beef, for example going to McDonald's, or Pizza Hut. They, together with Sikh children, also talked about special foods served to God (prasad), and communal meals at their place of worship.

> Interviewer: So like at home do you do any prayers or ceremonies?
> Girl: If it is say one of my God's birthday ... then we get up really early and my mum makes this thing ... and you pray at it ... boys pray at it ... and the girls just do that all ... And then like eat it ...
> Interviewer: Do you know the name of it?
> Girl: Prashad ...
> Interviewer: What does it taste like?
> Girl: It's got sugar in it it's sweet ...
> Interviewer: So it's a special food they you offer and pray and share?
> Girl: We eat it at the temple as well ...
> Interviewer: I've been in Sikh temples occasionally ... they often have meals ... together at the temple ... have you ever been to one of those?
> Girl: Yes we go and sit on the floor.
> Interviewer: What food do you eat?
> Girl: There are some chapattis ... And a chilli thing and a curry ... but there is different every Sunday that we go ...
> *(Sikh girl, School 1)*

When Christian and no religion children talked about food avoidance, it almost always involved food that they disliked, were allergic to or a few items like cat food, or slugs. A very small number mentioned giving up sweets for Lent. However, even with celebration foods such as turkey and Christmas pudding few of them indicated food had a religious significance in their own lives. Rather, they treated eating as a rather banal activity and food as a matter of personal choice.

Clearly food highlighted boundaries which meant that children from different communities of faith did not often eat together socially outside school. Muslims and non-Muslims were likely to visit different restaurants and take-aways and this would limit their social interaction outside school. For example, a weekend social trip arranged by the children in School 3 to McDonald's involved almost everyone apart from the Muslim boys and two girls who were visiting relatives. While our knowledge of the dynamics of the class suggests it is unlikely that the group of highly observant 'mosque boys' in this school would have gone, or even been invited, neither did the two Muslim boys who were members of the mixed 'lads' group. The Christian children, when discussing why the Muslims did not join in, speculated that they were not allowed 'because they maybe had to go to the mosque or temple or something'. There may of course be other explanations, such as the mixed gender of the group, the non-halal nature of the menu, or other family arrangements taking precedence. Yet it is significant that religious issues are interpreted by children here as placing a limit on informal social life.

Our key findings about life beyond the school are that:

- Religious identity and personal faith is not in itself a barrier to friendship. However, cross-cultural networks often did not continue into other contexts such as the home or neighbourhood.
- Children recognise this is the result of very different lifestyles that are shaped by religious differences, especially between highly observant Muslim children and less observant children.

5. Conclusions and implications

The evidence presented in this research shows that children aged from 9 to 11 who have experienced life in multi-faith neighbourhoods and schools understand many aspects of religious diversity, and are able to talk about it with interest and insight. The project has developed and used a range of research methods and tools which have allowed us to tap into a little studied area of children's lives, in a process which was enjoyable and educational for the researchers (and one hopes also for the children involved). It is to be hoped that this report has helped give children a voice on some important issues. Reflective evaluation and further development of these methods could well pay dividends for future research with children.

We hope that the three groups of key findings of the project summarised below provoke debate relevant to social scientists, policy-makers, teachers and religious organisations.

1. Children's religious identities and experiences are diverse and complex

Our research has revealed how children live in a complex social world characterised by religious diversity. Here they are called to do their identity work, resolving issues about who they are and to which communities they belong, and to negotiate social relationships with others. Within these processes many variables including age, gender, ethnicity and religious affiliation play a part as socially structured markers of difference, and children also relate to others on the basis of individual personality, current availability and shared interests. Religion itself is far from simple and can be perceived as having distinct elements. On the one hand, there is the social observance of religious practices and transmission of religious knowledge within particular traditions or communities of faith. On the other hand, there are the more private aspects of personal belief, theological speculation and spirituality in which all things are humanly and divinely possible. Children engage in both aspects of religious activity in a wide variety of different ways. The complexity of this situation means that no one should make assumptions, or apply stereotypes, to particular children or groups.

Complexity does not mean chaos or an absence of patterns worthy of investigation by sociologists of religion, ethnicity or childhood. There are several areas arising from this research which seem worthy of further theory building or research activity.

First of all, the limited coverage in this qualitative study means that the experience of many children is simply not touched on. Children in different regions or neighbourhoods, different types of school and from different religious and ethnic backgrounds, may have very different perspectives to the ones we interviewed. Furthermore, the small numbers in our sample make it impossible to extrapolate to whole populations of children of particular religious affiliations. Obviously this leads us to suggest there is a need for further research of a more widely representative type, although we should note that a sample survey adequate to represent the range of religious and ethnic diversity would be complex to design, and costly to carry out, might encounter particular fieldwork problems if working with children, and would be much more limited than in-depth interviews in terms of capturing the richness and nuances of children's own perspectives on the subject.

Second, the issue of children's identity development and the interplay of religion and ethnicity need further work. For example, we have not been able to look in detail at when and why children slip between using ethnic terms such as 'Asian' and religious terms such as 'Muslim' or 'Hindu' in labelling their own or other people's identities. In our project archive there are much data yet to be fully analysed which bear on these themes. It is hoped to find time and resources to look at this, and to write about it in ways which engage with the literature on ethnicity processes, on social cohesion and 'racialisation' of conflict and the debates about faith communities, religious discrimination and Islamophobia. It is to be hoped that our project's initial explorations of the field will encourage other social scientists to undertake research on these themes.

The fact that many of the children in our study come from ethnic minority communities who have migrated to and settled in Britain in living memory suggests a fruitful field for comparative investigation around issues of generational shift in patterns of religious observance and belief. Such work would be located in the broad area of sociology of religion, although it would also be of interest to sociologists of identity and ethnicity. In secularisation studies, debates about allegedly inexorable decline in believing and belonging, and the contrast between traditional modes of religion by obligation and a growing contemporary pattern of religion by consumer choice (Bruce 2002, Davie 1994, 2002) could be informed by this study. Thinking about religious diversity would widen the base of this field, which has tended to concentrate on trends in Christendom, while paying attention to the distinction between children being recipients of a tradition and actors exploring and developing their own faith and spirituality would also be worthwhile. Finally, the contemporary political context, in which religious issues and conflicts are resurgent, makes studies of the global and local dynamics of interreligious relations timely and important. The impact of these great issues on children and young people ought to be carefully monitored by research over time.

2. Education, diversity and social cohesion

Moving from research to policy and practice, mainly within the field of education (inside and outside school) some important issues emerge from this research. Within the United Nations Convention on the Rights of the Child, drawn up in 1989 and ratified by the UK in 1991, article 14 enshrines *the right of the child to freedom of thought, conscience and religion.* Our research and conversations with children convince us that such a right can be meaningful to children, and that they are capable of being religious and social actors in their own right, and of articulating views on issues that affect them, which ought to be listened to. Adults who see themselves as responsible for the religious socialisation of children, and organisations that organise religious instruction or other religious activities for children need to consider carefully what they are doing. There are some hard questions here about the power relationships between adults and children, the obligatory nature of some forms of religious instruction, and the methods used to encourage discipline and learning. At the very least adults need to think about whether some of the methods they use may be counterproductive and lead to resentment and alienation rather than the religious commitment they desire to see in the coming generation.

Current debates about the supposed failure of multiculturalism and the development of community cohesion policies need to take note of evidence about the role of schools and the voices of children. Primary schools are a key setting for children mixing across religions. The religious status of schools seems to be almost irrelevant from the children's perspective if the intake of pupils is religiously diverse. Many children said they enjoyed the opportunity to mingle and learn about other religions and cultures, although some expressed concern that they might struggle if their religious or ethnic group was a small minority within a school. The pattern and quality of relationships between pupils, in which religious difference may play as significant part as ethnicity or gender, may depend on local specifics of inter-group dynamics, such as the numerical balance of groups in the school and local community and the current state of community relations in the neighbourhood. Managing diversity, resolving conflicts and promoting greater understanding and tolerance between religious and ethnic groups is an area where schools face many challenges, but can make a major positive contribution.

School policy and practices can serve to promote cohesion and value diversity and in the schools we studied the children's accounts suggested there was much good practice. However, through listening to children's accounts of their life in school we have discovered some areas, such as singing, in which particular groups of children feel their religious concerns are not being fairly dealt with and of which school staff did not appear to be aware. The implication of this is that teachers should listen extensively and carefully to what children have to say about their experience and views of religion and not rely alone on what they learn from books, religious leaders or parents. Schools can appropriately build on the knowledge and experience of children, and of the local religious groups they may attend, in order to deliver high quality religious and citizenship education.

Friendship networks in primary school often transcend the boundaries of religion. However, children recognise that there are sometimes divisions and conflicts, which may be structured or exacerbated according to religious difference. Highly observant religious groups (not only Muslims) are sometimes marked and stigmatised as different from children who are less observant or do not follow a particular religion. The tendency to treat as 'normal' only children for whom religion is merely an optional, or part-time, aspect of their lives, must be resisted. Schools should regularly review their policies and practice, to ensure that all forms of religion are being treated with proper respect by staff and pupils, and that no children are marginalised or excluded from any aspect of school life because of religious factors.

Our findings suggest that very few children in these schools were concerned about the religious status of their current primary or future secondary school. Some children did express a preference for a faith-based school, and some were expecting to move on to one, but we need to understand better why this is the case, and the influence of the local context in which the supply side of the educational market, racism and religious intolerance may play a part. There is much as yet unanalysed data on this theme in our project archive, where children discuss the arguments for choosing particular schools or types of secondary education, and the role they played in family decision-making. We hope to have the opportunity to write more about this at a future date and believe there is scope, alongside an existing wide range of studies about children's transition to secondary schools, for new, more representative studies of children's experiences and perspectives on the various types of faith-based schools.

3. Religion may shape children's lifestyles in ways which divide and segregate groups

Religion (or the absence of it) may play a profound role in shaping children's lives, through social or moral obligation or in terms of cultural and ritual practice. Religious observance and instruction may take up a large proportion of children's time outside school. In our study this is especially the case for many of the most observant Muslims, although one could envisage many other communities of faith in the sectarian branches of Christianity, Judaism or Hinduism in which children might have a similar experience.

One of the impacts of this difference in lifestyle is that life beyond the school gate may be segregated by religion and that, even where children wish to mix, they may rarely have opportunity to do so. Our data and further research on this theme could profitably and critically engage with current academic and policy debates about social cohesion, and with those around the concept of social capital, and policy-makers' concern to measure and increase it, for the cause of urban renewal.

Slightly closer to everyday life, parents, religious leaders and other adults in children's lives would do well to consider the implications for society in the next generation. Is the desire to defend and maintain a cultural heritage and religious tradition at odds with a desire to live in a harmonious, tolerant, diverse and socially just society? If not, are there ways to ensure community cohesion amid religious diversity, without anyone having to compromise on deeply held beliefs and values on which their lifestyles are based? Perhaps the most hopeful note from this research is that we have discovered children who, in their everyday lives, are deeply engaged with these issues, aware of many of the opportunities and problems and already taking steps to work things out for themselves.

Glossary

This short glossary covers some religious terms used by the children in the original languages, Arabic, Urdu, Gujerati, Hindu, Punjabi. These are our own working definitions, rather than authoritative ones based on extensive research.

Islamic terms (based on Arabic)

Eid: one of the two main festival days in Islam. *Eid-ul-Fitr* is the celebration day marking the end of the Holy Month of fasting (*Ramadan* – often pronounced Ramzan). *Eid-ul-adha* occurs 40 days after the end of Ramadan, near the time specified for the *Haj* (pilgrimage to Mecca/Makkah). Known as the Festival of Sacrifice it is celebrated as a commemoration of Prophet Ibrahim's (PBUH) willingness to sacrifice his son for God, and is marked by the killing, cooking and sharing of a lamb.

Fajr: the earliest of the five daily prayers, just before dawn.

Hafiz: a Muslim recognised as having memorised the entire Arabic text of the Holy Quran.

Halal: is an Arabic word meaning lawful or permitted. The opposite of halal is *haram*, which means unlawful or prohibited. Halal and haram are universal terms that apply to all facets of life but most commonly the terms refer to food.

Jumma namaz: the Friday midday public prayers and sermon held at most mosques.

Namaz: the fivefold daily prayer times (the term *Salat* is also used).

Wud'u: sometimes spelled or pronounced *wudhu* or *wuzu*. The ritual acts of preparation Muslims are expected to make before doing namaz, or reading the Holy Quran, including both words and washing.

Zuhr: the second of the prayer times, scheduled around midday.

Sikh/Hindu terms derived from Sanskritic Languages

Diwali: Indian festival of lights, marking the New Year and usually celebrated in October.

Gurudwara: Sikh term for a local temple, literally meaning the door of the guru.

Mehndi: traditional decorative patterns, often painted in henna dye on the hands of women and girls, at times of celebration such as festivals and weddings.

Prasad/Prashad: food offered to God and/or ritually shared by devotees.

References

Bruce, S (2002) *God is Dead: Secularization in the West.* Oxford: Blackwell.

Cantle, T 'Community Cohesion: A Report of the Independent Review Team Chaired by Ted Cantle' (2001). http://www.homeoffice.gov.uk/comrace/cohesion/keydocs.html (accessed 25 April 2005).

Christensen, P and others (2003) 'Children in the city: home neighbourhood and community', *Progress in Human Geography*, 27, 5, 664–65.

Connolly, P (1998) *Racism, Gender Identities and Young Children: Social Relations in a Multi-Ethnic, Inner City Primary School.* London: Routledge.

Davie, G (1994) *Religion in Britain since 1945: Believing without Belonging.* Oxford: Blackwell.

Davie, G (2002) *Europe: The Exceptional Case.* London: Darton Longman and Todd.

Erricker, J, Ota, C and Erricker, C (eds) (2001) *Spiritual Education – Cultural, Religious and Social Differences: New Perspectives for the 21st Century.* Brighton: Academic Press.

Eslea, M and Mukhtar, K (2002) 'Bullying and racism among Asian schoolchildren in Britain', *Educational Research*, 42, 2, 207–17.

Farnell, R and others (2003) *'Faith' in Urban Regeneration? Engaging Faith Communities in Urban Regeneration.* Bristol: Joseph Rowntree Foundation/Policy Press.

Halstead, M (1994) 'Some reflections on the debate about music in Islam', *Muslim Educational Quarterly*, 12, 1, 51–62.

Hill, M and Tisdall, K (1997) *Children and Society.* Edinburgh: Addison Wesley Longman.

Jackson, R and Nesbitt, E (1993) *Hindu Children in Britain.* Stoke-on-Trent: Trentham Books.

James, A and others (1998) *Theorizing Childhood.* London: Polity Press.

London Borough of Redbridge (2003) 'SACRE Briefing Paper 4: Muslim Madrasahs in Redbridge', available from: Education Advisory Team, 255–59 High Road, Ilford IG1 1NN.

Mayall, B (2002) *Towards a Sociology of Childhood: Thinking from Children's Lives.* Buckingham: Open University Press.

Modood, T and others (1997) *Ethnic Minorities in Britain: Diversity and Disadvantage.* London: Policy Studies Institute.

Morrow, V (2001) *Networks and Neighbourhoods: Children's and Young People's Perspectives.* London: Health Development Agency.

Nesbitt, E (2000) 'The religious lives of Sikh children: a Coventry based study', Community Religions Monograph 7, Department of Theology and Religious Studies, University of Leeds.

Parker-Jenkins, M (1995) *Children of Islam: A Teacher's Guide to Meeting the Needs of Muslim Pupils.* Stoke-on-Trent: Trentham Books.

Smart, C and others (2001) *The Changing Experience of Childhood: Families and Divorce.* London: Polity Press with Blackwell.

Smith G (2004) 'Faith in community and communities of faith? Government rhetoric and religious identity in urban Britain', *Journal of Contemporary Religion*, 19, 2, 185–204.